Questions from the North; Answers from the South

James R. Elstad

Book cover designed by: Elizabyth Harrington

Entire book electronically assembled by Mary D. Scott
www.SpiritDrivenEvents.com

Library of Congress Cataloging-in-Publication Data available upon request.
ISBN – 13: 978-1517449865
ISBN – 10: 1517449863

Printed in the United States of America

October 2015

DEDICATION

To: My late wife Bonniejean, my best friend and supporter; my children: (the lights of my life) Amber, Shannon, Peter, and Chris; my grandchildren (the shining stars in my life): Laura, Emily, Victoria, Juliet, and Liam; the family I grew up with: Linda, Rita, David, and Donna; and most of all to my Mom and Dad, who made me what I am.

ACKNOWLEDGEMENTS

Editors: Mike Foley, Diane Moore, Bard Folk; **Critique Group:** Moonstruck Café, 9 Bridges. **Interviewees:** Dr. Charles E. Baker; Greg Eanes; Antoine Fletcher, Michael T. Griffith; Stanley K. Lott; Lochlainn Seabrook; Dr. Edward C. Smith; H.V. Traywick, Jr.; and Nelson Winbush.

ABOUT THE AUTHOR

Jim was born on Staten Island, NY, and was raised in Southern California. While in junior high he started writing stories, but it wasn't until he joined the High Desert Chapter, California Writer's Club that he really started to focus on his work.

Jim retired from active duty with the California Army National Guard which completed a twenty-eight year career, which included a three-year enlistment in the U.S. Marines.

Currently Jim is working on an alternate history of the 1860s and plans a prequel to the "Comes the" series.

TABLE OF CONTENTS

Preface

Why was the Civil War fought if it wasn't to "emancipate" the slaves?

During the three years I've been selling books I've had many readers ask about the causes of the Civil War. The majority of the people seem to believe slavery and racism were the main causes.

As I've conducted research for my novels I've continued to search. I started by contacting four people, two black descendants of slaves and two white descendants of southern aristocracy I've met during the past three years. I also discovered DVDs and CDs that discussed the Civil War from the point of view of both black and white Southerners. I sent inquiries to each Southerner I knew and reviewed the material I had gathered for answers to the issues my readers were asking.

As the answers came in I continued to surf the internet for information that would tie-up loose ends. In this book, I have covered:

1. Why Do Southerners Keep Fighting The Civil War Over and Over?
2. Wasn't The South Responsible For Slavery?
3. Shouldn't the South Pay Reparations?
4. Why is Robert E. Lee revered so much?
5. What Legal Standing Was There To Secede?
6. Wasn't the North justified in doing whatever was necessary to free the slaves?
7. Didn't the Southern States Just want to control the Union?
8. Didn't the CSA VP Believe that Slavery was the Cause of the Civil War?
9. How has History Led US to Where We are Today?

Please note the tone of "voice" used by some Southerners may sound harsh. My intent is for this book is a platform for them to express their point of view.

What I see in society today is both sides of the political spectrum arguing and not listening to their opponent. What I've come to realize is the roots of our problems today go back to the beginning of our nation. If we don't resolve the core issues we're in for a blood bath worse than what we saw in 1861-1865.

One - Why Do Southerners Keep Fighting The Civil War Over and Over?

This is the first question I received almost three years ago. I was at dinner with friends. As we discussed my first book, "Comes the Southern Revolution," My friend couldn't understand why Southerners still get angry about how the North portrays the Civil War. I asked Mr. Lochlainn Seabrook, a very articulate and prolific southern author, what his response would be.

> "This is just another Yankee myth to try and obscure the truth of the matter. We Southerners are indeed still fighting, but obviously not the War itself. What we are doing is struggling to achieve the one and only goal that our conservative, Confederate ancestors fought and died for: strict constitutionalism, which in turn infers a small limited central government, states' rights, and personal liberty."[i]

Continuing with that line of reasoning, Mr. H.V. Traywick said this in his e-mail:

> "So the North provoked the South into firing the first shot, blockaded the Confederate coasts, and marched her armies across the South to the tune of the Puritanical and militantly intolerant Battle Hymn of the Republic – burning and pillaging and raping and killing – until she drove the Southern States back into the Union."[ii]

It seems to feel the northern actions were taken in two parts, probably not by design, but there is a definite watershed. Northern actions against the South during the conflict and actions taken after the conflict supposedly ended. It seems to me that with all the violence that's occurred, caused by both sides, in the past one-hundred-fifty years that no one could say the issues have been fully resolved.

> "Then - by the Reconstruction Acts that dis-franchised Southern intelligence and enfranchised Southern ignorance under the control of unscrupulous and predatory Northern carpetbaggers and demagogues propped up by Federal bayonets – the North passed Amendments that effectively gutted the Constitution of its federative nature, and put the Federal Government under her unlimited control (18)."[iii]

Traywick goes on to state his belief that after the southern issue was resolved in the northern mind, the North turned its attention west.

> "With the stumbling blocks of the South and the Constitution finally out of the way of her ambitions, the North then sent Sherman, Sheridan and Custer out to the Great Plains to tend to the Indians, who were in the way of her transcontinental railroads. (The South's accounts of these genocidal incendiaries are underscored ten-fold by the Indians' subsequent accounts in Dee Brown's *Bury My Heart at Wounded Knee* (19).)

> But this doesn't look too good on the pages of a fourth grade history book or in a National Park Service film presentation, so the North's war of conquest must be cloaked in robes of morality and turned into a war of liberation. To the victor belong the spoils, and the "Official History Book" - written by "Court Historians," taught in public schools, and romanticized endlessly on the TV and movie screens - is one of the spoils of war."[iv]

My Take:

The Southerners have never denied they lost the war. I can see their point. It's one thing to express your point of view; it's another to remove the other's side's point-of-view completely. They do not want to keep the Northern point-of-view out of the history books; they want the Southern point-of-view put back in.

Two - Wasn't The South Responsible For Slavery?

This is the second most common question I've been asked. It's as if people assume the southern aristocracy started slavery, and was responsible for everything associated with it. I shouldn't be surprised about that. I was born in New York, raised in Southern California, and graduated with a BA in U.S. History from California State University, Northridge.

While my professors covered more than slavery, they and the textbooks they required us to study emphasized slavery as the main cause. I remember coming away with the impression that: "All slaves were uneducated; picked cotton; and were brutally beaten every day."

How bad was it, really? Here in the 21st Century, it's rightfully considered an abomination. For many citizens in the pre-Civil War era, I can't say antebellum because we're including the entire USA, slavery was legal, it was a way of life. It appears that citizens on both sides of the Mason-Dixon Line were involved in the slavery business from "procurement" (slave auctions) to slave catching (there were several Native American tribes active in the trade, some as owners of white, black, and Native American slaves). "Many runaway slaves, when they realized a Catawba tribesman from South Carolina were on their trail, would turn around and go back rather than face falling into the hands of such a fierce warrior."[v]

That's not to say that slavery wasn't a horrible experience for the slave. But when Union troops arrived to "liberate" them, why don't we have a record of slaves rejoicing and revolting against their oppressors? As a white man I can only imagine what it would be

4

like to own or be a slave. When I have dinner or go to a party with my friends who are black, the thought crosses my mind of how awful the institution really was. Especially when I consider the slaves were humans, they had feelings and emotions. Then when I ponder the thought that most slave owners treated their slaves humanely I wonder how the two sides could come together. Then when we take into account that with only two percent of the whites owned slaves, why was it such an emotional issue?

A concept that comes to mind is that many slave owners treated their slaves as family; they worked next to them in the fields, and shared hardships with them. Another point is that when the Southern men went off to war, who did they leave in charge? The women and slaves; if slaves were so mistreated why didn't they take advantage of the opportunity and revolt?

One point that Griffith brings out is that:

> "Several northern emancipation laws included clauses that decreed that slave children would not be free until they were in their twenties. Pennsylvania is a good case in point. The state abolished slavery in 1780. Yet, slave children who were born a few days before the passage of the abolition act had to wait over twenty years before the law actually set them free. Of course, this gave their owners the chance to recover the cost of raising them, at the very least."[vi]

He also noted that:

> "Most of the northern states that abolished slavery before the Civil War did so gradually and provided various forms of compensation to slaveholders."[vii]

Northerners owned the slave-trading ships (which flew under the American flag), controlled the slave markets, and their textile mills and manufacturing endeavors benefited from slave labor long after they started on their righteous abolitionist trail. There were Northerners who had slaves up until the end of the Civil War (citizens of Maryland, Delaware, Kentucky, and Missouri), many of the Union Army's General Staff owned slaves that served them while their supposed goal was to free the southern slaves.

Southerners for whatever reason willingly participated in the beginnings of slavery and benefited from the labor of blacks. True most Southerners didn't own slaves, but it's hard to deny that all southerners benefited when their economy grew because of slavery.

Still another point to bring out is that many slaves fought alongside their masters and their sons; so many that after hostilities ceased each state had a procedure and forms for a "Colored Man's Pension."[viii]

I recall a statement that Traywick made, "The respective labor systems of the antagonists were just as irrelevant in this conflict as in any other war of conquest."[ix]

In December of 2012, as I conducted a book signing at the Los Angeles Air Force Base Exchange, I called a passerby over to my table. When he stood in front of me he stabbed the cover for "Comes the Southern Revolution" and said, "I'd rather have Hitler and the Nazis come back rather than him." He walked away before I could find out why he felt such a strong hatred.

I can only surmise that he believed Robert E. Lee, and others of the southern aristocracy, were evil and supported the brutal institution of slavery.

That event brought me to: "Where did the institution of "American" slavery come from?

In June 1997, when I first thought of the premise for "Comes the Southern Revolution" until now, I really started studying U.S. History in general and the Civil War in particular. I've come to realize the logistics of managing an enterprise as large as slavery was not a "mom and pop" operation. It was a global effort.

They had to procure slaves from somewhere, and then they needed to be transported to market. That would entail feeding and some means of transportation, and care would have to be paid for. How did it start? Who was responsible?

In my research I haven't heard of a legend that a group of southerners sitting around their kitchen table planning on how to enslave their fellow human beings. In fact one of the first legal cases regarding slavery was in 1650s Virginia. That case was a ruling in favor of a black man named Anthony Johnson who laid claim to some slaves.[x]

Suffice it to say that slavery has been around for thousands of years. In the beginning most slaves came from Africa, many of the white slaves started off as "indentured servants" and came from Ireland whose term of service never expired. There were blacks and American Indians who owned slaves (black, Indians, and white).

From the 1650s to the early 1800s almost all slaves were from Africa and were provided by Arab slavers. The slaves were transported to South America, the Caribbean, and the U.S. (all of the American colonies allowed slavery). I found evidence that "southerners weren't responsible for slavery" in a book called "Generations of Captivity" by Ira Berlin:

> "Black life on mainland North America originated not in Africa or America but in the netherworld between the two continents. Along the periphery of the Atlantic — first in Africa, then Europe, and finally in the Americas—it was a product of the momentous meeting of Africans and Europeans and then their equally fateful rendezvous with the peoples of the New World."[xi]

To answer those questions would take more time and space than we have in this book. For an in-depth look at the issue read "Everything You Were Taught about American Slavery is Wrong, Ask A Southerner."[xii]

In the past three years no one has come to me advocating that we return to slavery. Yet when I start talking to some people the first comment they make is: "Your book doesn't suggest we should go back to slavery does it?" The feeling seems to be that the only reason the South had to secede was to continue slavery.

According to Lott, (who happens to be descended from slaves) in the manuscript for his book, "Lincoln and the U.S. Government (The Stone Cold Facts),"

> "In 1620 the first African landed in Jamestown, Virginia. Slavery began in all thirteen colonies that became the United States. . . Slavery first existed in twelve of the thirteen colonies but was legal in all thirteen. The British Common Law in the colonies protected Slavery. Some of our law system was derived from the British Common Law. It naturalized the custom of African nations of treating slaves as property."[xiii]

Lott explained that:

> "Treaties with foreign nations specially stipulated for the indemnification (payment) for the loss of the slaves. This was done by Jay's Treaty, the Treaty of Ghent, and the treaty for the purchase of Louisiana recognized and protected the rights of property in slaves. This shows how important slavery was to the Colonial and Northern interests. It was officially recognized and protected by our very own U.S. Constitution.[xiv]

When we take into account that "civilized" nations were making treaties to regulate the slave trade, this is far beyond the scope of the southern aristocracy and especially the local plantation owner.

Now we need to look at who transported the slaves? I haven't found one source documenting that a southern slave holder/owner or southern businessman owned a ship that was outfitted to transport slaves.

The fact that Northern interests kept slavery is demonstrated in the United States Constitution:

"No Person held to Service or Labour in one State, under the Laws thereof, escaping into another, shall, in Consequence of any Law or Regulation therein, be discharged from such Service or Labour, but shall be delivered up on Claim of the Party to whom such Service or Labour may be due."[xv]

My Take:

As I've been working on this manuscript I realized that the Northern Abolitionists are like a reformed alcoholic. They feel self-righteous because they've been able to deal with their demons and are insistent that others with the same problem snap their fingers, take their advice, and obey their rules. That brings to mind Jesus' words:

"And why do you look at the speck in your brother's eye, but do not consider the plank in your own eye? Or how can you say to your brother, Let me remove the speck from your eye', and look, a plank is in your own eye."[xvi]

Three - Shouldn't the South Pay Reparations?

A few readers/passersby have asked me about reparations from the "South" to descendants of slaves. In retrospect their question could have been more for its shock value than a serious inquiry. But on its face value they seem to be stating that since the southern aristocracy was responsible for slavery in the South, that their descendants who have benefited from that evil curse should make amends.

My dictionary defines "Reparations" as:

1. "The act or process of making amends for a wrong."
2. "Something done or money paid to make amends or compensate for a wrong."
3. "Compensation or remuneration, as for damage or economic loss, required from a nation defeated in war."
4. "The act or process of repairing or the condition of being repaired."

Four Southerners responded to this question. Mr. Nelson Winbush, grandson of Louis Nelson, who as a fourteen-year old slave, went to fight with his best friends, who happened to be his master's two sons. During the conflict he was the company cook, and chaplain. Winbush told me:

> On Sunday mornings the Union and Rebel troops would declare a truce; the Union soldiers would cross the battle front, and participate in Sunday services. After evening services they'd go back to their camp and on Monday the battle would resume.[xvii]

Winbush informed me that:

> Louis must've done more than cook and preach, because after the war he was given a "Colored Man's Pension" from the State of Tennessee,[xviii] blacks owned slaves in Louisiana, Mississippi, Virginia, and the Carolinas. Many of these slaves went to war alongside their masters, freedmen, and other slaves.[xix]

Another source of information regarding black Confederate soldiers is Greg Eanes book: "Virginia's Black Confederates."

> "Aaron Burton, one of the most notable blacks, started the war as: "a servant and coachman" to A.D. Mosby, father of the soon-to-be famed guerilla leader. Burton reportedly remained with Mosby throughout the entire war. He is mentioned prominently in Mosby's published Memoirs and as well as letters."[xx]

A black man must have accomplished much to be mentioned in such an important person's recollection of the war. Mosby commented on Burton's bravery when he mentioned him in a letter to his sister:

> "The small squad surprised and charged at an equal number of Federals who ran and ended up stampeding the entire regiment "thinking all of Stuart's cavalry were on them." Mosby continued to write: "Aaron thinks himself quite a hero, though he does not want to come again in such disagreeable proximity to a bombshell."[xxi]

Virginia is the second state that I found that provided a pension for black veterans (freedmen and slaves). I'm sure there were others.

A side note on the issue of blacks serving in either army is that the Union Army was segregated with white officers. The Rebel Army didn't keep track of race on their enlistment records. Their units included all races.

The next Southerner to respond to this question is Mr. Lochlainn Seabrook. Seabrook has many ancestors who fought for the South, and a few who were hanged for supporting the South. He's written over thirty-one books on the "War of Northern Aggression" and Antebellum issues, and has many more in the works. His answer to this question is:

> "Additionally, Portugal introduced African slavery to Europe, Spain introduced it to the Americas, and both the Dutch and the English introduced it to North America. Furthermore, Africa herself was practicing various barbaric forms of slavery on her own people for thousands of years prior to the introduction of the transatlantic slave trade, and indeed was instrumental in opening up the slave trade with Arabia and later Europe and America. Are not all of these regions and nations also culpable? And who is to pay reparations to the modern day descendants of the 1.5 million whites who were held in slavery in Africa during the late 1700s and 1800s?"[xxii]

Seabrook also mentioned:

> "Why should it [the South pay reparations] when American slavery was launched in the North, the region that practiced slavery far longer than the South and which possessed far more slave owners and slaves than the South well into the early 1800s? One must also consider that America had thousands of black and Indian slaveholders as well, many who owned not just black slaves, but also white slaves."[xxiii]

The last Southerner, Mr. Michael T. Griffith states: "Newport, Rhode Island, was one of the two main ports for the American slave trade. The other main port was Boston, Massachusetts."[xxiv]

Two other complications come to mind:

1. The odds are that today many descendants of slaves from the American past are also descendants of slave owners (white, black, or American Indian).

2. From the vehement attitude of many today would they even hold those who didn't own slaves but fought for the rebels, responsible for reparations?

To close out this question, we should remember that it would be impossible to track down all perpetrators of the African slave trade and then force them to pay reparations. Some might say that when criminals are caught society doesn't wait for everyone to be apprehended before the wheels of justice start turning. In the same way society needs to exact payment from those who can be proven to be descendants of those responsible.

But where would the money come from? The government? Companies? Plantations, organizations that are still in business? That would be difficult, since many members of each of the above have no ancestral connection with the African slave trade.

I have a brother-in-law who moved from Southern California to North Carolina. What about a descendant of a Chinese-American who immigrated to Alabama in the late 1800s? Should their tax money go toward reparations? The list is endless. Should those who have no ancestral connection to the African slave trade be forced to have their tax money spent on 'reparations?' What about a shareholder from Europe who invests in a southern company that is proven to be 'culpable' in the African slave trade? Who will go to the investors of today's shipping companies who benefited from the African slave trade and exact payment of reparations?

My Take:

It doesn't seem as if there is any way to be fair and single out those who "should" be required to pay reparations. How could it be sorted out? Would everyone who wanted to make a claim have to submit to a DNA test? Would descendants of black and Native American slave holders/owners have to pay reparations? Would people of color who are found to have both slave and slave holder/owner DNA in their veins have to pay reparations to themselves? How can you guarantee the written records are

13

accurate and reliable enough to use them as a benchmark for making a determination?

Four - Why is Robert E. Lee revered so much?

In 2014 I met a Northern civil war reenactor who discussed Robert E. Lee at length. His main argument was that: "all officers of the day, as now, swear an oath to uphold the Constitution of the United States of America. And even though Robert E. Lee claimed to be a 'Christian,' the fact that he violated his oath;" and, in this Northerner's mind, the fact that he owned slaves, "made him a very despicable man."

The longer we talked the more I realized that he was not interested in discussing the facts. His mind was made up and he was judging Robert E. Lee with 2014 standards.

I could have stayed and debated the issue with him, but sometimes I can tell it would be a waste. What I would've wanted him to understand is that in the 1860s most people thought of themselves as citizens of their state more than a citizen of the United States of America.

Dr. Edward C. Smith supported my belief that General Lee considered himself a Virginian more than an American when he said:

> "Two of Lee's ancestors signed the Declaration of Independence. His father was George Washington's Chief of Staff. His wife was George Washington's step-great-granddaughter. Leaving the Union Army, having served it for so long, having served as Superintendent of West Point, having been a war hero in the Mexican-American War, it must've been devastating for him to resign his commission. Remember back then one's loyalty went to your State first,

the United States second. When someone (from the North or South) said "my country" they meant their State."[xxv]

I realize that this last statement, even though it showed Robert E. Lee's Virginian roots, doesn't prove why General Lee was more loyal to Virginia. A while ago I read a news article by Doug Bandow, where he stated:

> "When his home state of Virginia voted to secede, then Col. Lee, who turned down Lincoln's offer of command of the Northern armies, explained: "I can anticipate no greater calamity for the country than dissolution of the Union. ... Still, a Union that can only be maintained by swords and bayonets, and in which strife and civil war are to take the place of brotherly love and kindness, has no charm for me.""[xxvi]

This seems to show the conflict the General must have gone through. And in the end he sided with his country, "Virginia."

Another incorrect assumption my reenactor made, is that General Lee was a slave owner. Smith again had the answer:

> "Lee's 300 blacks were listed on census records as 'our people' not slaves. Almost all of them were skilled craftsmen. All were literate.[xxvii]

Another interesting aspect was brought out by Seabrook when he responded:

> "As for Lee being a "slave owner," no one who has honestly and objectively studied the Lee family would ever make this statement. Unlike Yankee hero Ulysses S. Grant, Lee never personally owned slaves. He did inherit a small group of black servants from his wife Mary Anna Custis, which, upon marriage, she had inherited from her father (as was the custom in both the North and the South at the time).[xxviii]

That is quite different from the lessons I was taught in high school and college. At this point in my research I was wondering what other lies had I been told and what is wrong with learning the truth?

"In addition, General Lee liberated all of the Custis family slaves before Lincoln issued his fake and illegal Emancipation Proclamation on January 1, 1863. Of course, Lee's actions are just what one would expect from a Virginian, the state in which the American abolition movement was born. For more on this fascinating and amazing man, I direct the reader to my books The Old Rebel: Robert E. Lee As He Was Seen By His Contemporaries, and The Quotable Robert E. Lee."[xxix]

Seabrook is upfront when he talks about who was the traitor to the original Constitution.

"General Lee was one of the finest examples of American patriotism, authentic Christianity, and Southern traditionalism that this country has ever seen or will ever see. And this is precisely why traditional Southerners and enlightened non-Southerners love and honor him. In Lee's day, while Northerners considered themselves "Americans," our independent-minded southern ancestors considered themselves "Southerners," freedom-loving men and women who viewed their home state as their true "country." And it was for this reason that when Lincoln decided to invade the South, Lee and millions of other Southerners abandoned the U.S.A. and swore allegiance to their individual states.

And let us note that Lee's decision was not without anguish. He loved the original American government and was loath to renounce it. In the end, after hearing of Lincoln's plans to over-ride the Constitution [Author's note: A matter for Congress, not Executive Order] and undermine the government of the Founding Fathers, he felt he had no choice but to leave the Union in order to fight for their preservation against an enemy hell-bent on obliterating

17

them." To us here in the South, it is not our region that is guilty of "treason," it is the North for seeking to overturn the Ninth and Tenth Amendments."[xxx]

Griffith had a few comments about General Lee and slavery.

"The Confederacy's leading general, Robert E. Lee, believed slavery was "a moral and political evil." During the war, General Lee advocated freeing all slaves who served in the Confederate Army, along with their families. He said these measures should be followed by the gradual emancipation of all other slaves."[xxxi]

Smith portrays the Lee family's attitude toward their slaves.

"As was mentioned earlier the blacks living and serving with the Lee family were listed on the census as: "our people" not slaves. Agnes Lee, Robert E. Lee's daughter, would teach her 'ebony scholars' how to read and write on the estate."[xxxii]

Another aspect of the relationship the Lee family had with the blacks who lived at Arlington, was shown in the interaction between Mrs. Lee and Salina Gray in 1863 when the Yankees were advancing toward them.

"Salina Gray was Mrs. Lee's best friend. In 1863 Mrs. Lee handed the keys to Arlington to Mrs. Gray and told her the Union Army was coming over and this 1100 acre plantation is left in your care. They may try to do damage to the property. You must try to protect it. Mrs. Lee didn't return until 1873 (8 years after the war was over, and a few months before she died). Salina was still living there until she died in 1907. This story was repeated in many households and plantations throughout the South."[xxxiii]

These three examples of how the Lee family treated the blacks under their care show that they were not racist, in fact Smith mentions that after General Lee became President of Washington

College many of the blacks from their home in Arlington followed them and served the General as freemen and freewomen.[xxxiv]

If General Lee was the racist some portray him to be, why did so many of his former slaves revere him so much?

From what I've found, in addition to the quotes mentioned above, the Lee's weren't the exception in how they treated their slaves and the blacks who stayed on after they were freed, prior to the beginning of the Civil War weren't the exception either.

My Take:

Logically when the white men went off to war, who was it who stayed behind to manage the family business? If blacks, freed and slave had been treated as harshly as was portrayed in the miniseries "Roots" there would have been violent slave uprisings as soon as the men departed. Instead for the entire length of the Civil War, the white women and black slaves and freed men and women supported the southern war effort.

Smith explains why in one word: "patriotism."[xxxv]

Those who portray General Lee as racist and evil are guilty of judging 19th century citizens by 21st century mores.

Five - What Legal Standing Was There To Secede?

Of all the questions I've been asked this is the one that carries the least amount of emotion. Many northerners I've spoken with assume that once a state joined the union that it lost its sovereignty.

On the floor of the U.S. Congress Lott found a quote validating the position that prior to the Civil War most residents thought of themselves as citizens of their state first, then as an "American."

> "You have got the territory in all its length and breadth, North and South, East and West, and we have non to give unless we give up to you that strip of seashore that we own, extending three miles from the coast; for I believe that is the only place where the Federal Flag (American Flag) waves outside of a state, where you have not got everything that you have ever claimed for slavery."[xxxvi]

In this quote the Congressman states that all his state owns is a strip of seashore and three miles out to sea. Outside of that the Federal government has jurisdiction. The comment was not disputed by any other member of Congress. This would imply that the sovereignty of the States was accepted.

When I listened to Griffith's lecture on "A Southern View of the Civil War," I was interested in his comment that in July 1861 that Congress passed a resolution that the North was not waging war to end slavery but only to preserve the Union. I skimmed the Congressional Globe for July 1861 and found that on July 25, 1861 the House of Representatives unanimously passed the "Crittenden-Johnson Resolution which stated:

". . . the war is being waged for the reunion of the states and not to interfere with the institutions of the South, namely slavery."[xxxvii]

Another fact that supports the sovereignty of the states is that when British General Cornwallis surrendered to the Revolutionaries at the end of the Revolutionary War, he surrendered to each of the individual states, not to a national government.[xxxviii]

Along the same line of reasoning, Griffith states:

"The states were sovereign and independent long before the federal government was formed in 1789. In 1776, in the Declaration of Independence, Thomas Jefferson described the thirteen American colonies as "free and independent states." He also said they had "full Power to levy War, conclude Peace, contract Alliances, establish Commerce, and to do all other Acts and Things which independent States may of right do."[xxxix]

Griffith continues with his explanation of why it was legal for the South to secede.

"The Articles of Confederation, ratified by the states in 1781, eight years before the federal government was formed, said, "Each state retains its sovereignty, freedom, and independence." Obviously, the states could not have retained their sovereignty and independence if they didn't already possess them."[xl]

In light of the last quote, it is amazing that President Lincoln would "claim that the states had never been sovereign outside the Union, and that the Constitution was ratified by the people as a whole, i.e., by the people acting as "one people," and not in any sense by the states. These claims are contrary to the facts of history and to the Constitution itself, yet they are repeated in numerous history books."[xli]

As to Lincoln's claim that the Constitution was ratified by the people all we need to do is look at "Article 7" of the U.S. Constitution which states:

> "The ratification of the Conventions of nine states shall be sufficient for the establishment of this Constitution between the states so ratifying the same."[xlii]

Griffith adds his take on the issue:

> "In practice the legislature of each state called a ratification convention, the citizens of the state voted for delegates to the convention, and those delegates decided whether or not to ratify the Constitution. No state's convention was binding on any other state."[xliii]

This brings up and interesting point. What if only nine of the original colonies had chosen to ratify the U.S. Constitution? Logic says the remaining four states would be sovereign nations and separate from the United States of America. Therefore, since nothing in the US Constitution takes away a state's sovereignty, it would seem that any state that ratified the Constitution would still retain its sovereignty.

Another supporter of the sovereignty of the states is:

> "Samuel Chase, a signer of the Declaration of Independence and a justice on the Supreme Court under George Washington, said the colonies were "each of them. . . a sovereign and independent state" and "that each of them had a right to govern itself by its own authority and its own laws, without any control from any other power on earth" (Ware v. Hylton, 1796, 3 Dallas 224)."[xliv]

Griffith mentions that even prior to the Declaration of Independence the colonies were sovereign.

> "In 1774, founding father James Wilson said the colonies, even as members of the British Empire, were "distinct states, independent of each other," and that therefore they

22

had the right to control their own internal affairs ("Considerations on the Nature and Extent of the Legislative Authority of the British Parliament," 1774)."[xlv]

What would be the reason for opponents of secession to deny the sovereignty of the states? Griffith answers that in the quote below:

"Opponents of secession denied the sovereignty of the states because they realized that if the states had ever been sovereign outside the Union, then they had the natural right to peacefully leave the Union."[xlvi]

James Madison, Founding Father, signer of the Declaration of Independence, stated:

"Each State, in ratifying the Constitution, is considered as a sovereign body, independent of all others, and only to be bound by its own voluntary act. . ." He "made it clear that the people would not be acting as one nation. He said that ratification would be a federal and not a national act," that would be "the act of the people, as forming so many independent States, not as forming one aggregate nation."[xlvii]

Madison has quite an impressive resume: helped draft the U.S. Constitution, the Bill of Rights, co-founded the Democratic-Republican Party, and was the fourth President of the United States.

Madison was not the only founding father to have this point-of-view.

"In the Kentucky resolution of 1798 Jefferson said the following: Resolved, that the several States composing the United States of America are not united on the principle of unlimited submission to their general government; but that by compact under the style and title of a Constitution for the United Sates and of amendments thereto, they constituted a general government for special purposes, delegated to that government certain definite powers, reserving each State to

23

itself, the residuary mass of right to their own self-government; and that whensoever the general government assumes undelegated powers, its acts are unauthorative, void and of no force: That to this compact each State acceded as a State. . . . That the government created by this compact was not made the exclusive or final judge of the extent of the powers delegated to itself. . . but that as in all other cases of compact among parties having no common Judge, each party has an equal right to judge for itself, as well of infractions as of the mode and measure of redress (The Kentucky Resolutions, 1798)."[xlviii]

Griffith came up with an interesting point:

"Thomas Jefferson warned that America was not founded on the idea of unlimited submission by the states to the national government, and that the national government should not be the judge of its own powers."[xlix]

There are more quotes that could be cited, however, why belabor the point? It appears obvious the states were considered sovereign by the framers of the US Constitution. Apparently the legality of secession was not lost to many northern citizens, particularly journalists.

"Horace Greeley expressed the feelings of many Northern citizens on this issue. Greeley was a prominent Republican, an abolitionist, and an influential newspaper publisher. Greeley said the following shortly after Lincoln was elected:

We hold with Jefferson, to the inalienable right of communities to alter or abolish forms of government that have become oppressive or injurious; and, if the Cotton States [the Deep South states] shall decide that they can do better out of the Union than in it, we insist on letting them go in peace. . . . And, whenever a considerable section of our Union shall deliberately resolve to go out, we shall resist all coercive measures designed to keep her in. We hope never to live in a republic where one section is pinned to the residue by bayonets."[l]

Historian Henry C. Perkins studied four-hundred-ninety-five Northern newspaper editorials that were written from late 1860 to mid-1861 and found that the right of secession was not disputed:[li]

> "During the weeks following the election [1860 Presidential election between Abraham Lincoln and Stephen Douglas], editors of all parties assumed that secession as a constitutional right was not in question. . . . On the contrary, the southern claim to a right of peaceable withdrawal was countenanced [accepted] out of reverence for the natural law principal of government by consent of the governed."[lii]

The final quote in this section comes from Seabrook.

> "In the mid-1800s the states' rights of both accession (joining the U.S.) and secession (leaving the U.S.) were taken for granted by both the American populace and American statesmen. In fact, secession was the most discussed political concept in America right up to and beyond Lincoln's War. It was so taken for granted that the Founders did not even bother including any obvious reference to it in the Constitution. Instead, they gave tacit mention of it in the all important Bill of Rights as Amendments Nine and Ten."[liii]

I found this particularly fascinating. In all my northern education I was led to believe that the idea of secession was a new concept generated by Southerners. To me this is one of many new facets of the conflict that came to light. Seabrook continues:

> "While critics of secession decry the actions of the Southern states in 1860 and 1861 as "unconstitutional" and "treasonous," they neglect to mention that there is nothing in the Constitution prohibiting secession. And in fact, this right was upheld by nearly every member of the Founding Generation, as well as most of our presidents, right up to our

fifteenth chief executive, James Buchanan. It was our demagogic sixteenth president, big government Liberal Abraham Lincoln, who was the first to derail the Constitution, murder countless thousands of Americans, and nearly bankrupt the U.S. Treasury in an attempt to destroy the right of secession."[liv]

My Take:

According to the sources quoted in this chapter, there was a large amount of northern support for allowing the southern states to secede. This begs the question, how and why did we get to the point we are today where the only issues taught in our schools regarding the causes of the civil war are slavery and the brutality of the southern aristocracy against the human beings they held in captivity?

We'll discuss more of that later, for now it appears that secession was openly debated on both sides of the Mason-Dixon Line, and President Lincoln forced many newspapers out of business or arrested any journalist whom he thought supported the South's right to peacefully secede from the Union.[lv]

Six - Wasn't the North justified in doing whatever was necessary to free the slaves?

Readers who asked this question seem to believe the premise furthered by Northerners and promoted by Hollywood and television. The idea that all slaves picked cotton, all were illiterate, and all slave owners were brutal and abused their slaves.

It's as if a culture so brutal as to treat fellow humans so poorly deserved to be destroyed. Proof Northerners in the 1860's felt that way is demonstrated by the fact that sixty-eight Republican Congressman supported an advertisement for books, titled:

> "The Impending Crisis of The South, by Hinton Helper."[lvi]
> Two other books were: "The Stupid Masses of the South" and "Revolution. . . . Violently If We Must."[lvii]

All three advocated a slave revolt and the killing of southern whites.

Is it any wonder southern leaders did not trust their Northern counter-parts? Some responders to my inquiries have other reasons that shed light on the northern motives.

Griffith says:

> "As the Confederates themselves pointed out, any nation would regard it as an aggressive, hostile act for another nation to send an uninvited force into one of its harbors to resupply a garrison that had occupied an island in that harbor without permission. If the British had seized an island in New York harbor shortly after the colonies had declared their independence, the Patriots would have viewed

27

this as an act of aggression. And if the British had sent an armed naval convoy to attempt to resupply the occupying force, the Patriots would have regarded this as a hostile, provocative act as well."[lviii]

Traywick made a good point about southern intentions regarding slavery when he told me:

"The fallacies of Lincoln's accusations are readily apparent. The Southern States – far from withdrawing from the Union in order to expand the territorial limits of slavery - essentially *gave up* their claims to the territories rather than live under a Northern despotism, and thereby *restricted* their avenues for the expansion [of] slavery!

This not only brought about what Lincoln said was the Federal Government's sole object – to restrict slavery's expansion - it went most of the way towards peacefully removing slavery from the United States altogether!"[lix]

It appears that the last quote would take away slavery as a motive for the conflict. But what about the issue of who started the fight? Who really fired the first shot?

"As for rending the Union, "even by war," I would ask: Who rebuffed Southern diplomatic overtures of peace from December 1860 to April 1861? Whose garrison committed the first act of war by spiking the guns at Ft. Moultrie and slipping into Ft. Sumter in the dark of night in direct violation of the truce then in effect? And who deceived the South diplomatically until he could send a powerfully armed armada to Charleston to provoke the South into firing the first shot?"[lx]

When I first read this response, I wondered how it applied to this question. Then I realized if the Union's (really Mr. Lincoln's) main object was freeing the slaves why did he wait years to free the slaves? Why did slave owners in Maryland, Kentucky, Delaware, and Missouri not have to free their slaves when the war started? Then when the Emancipation Proclamation was enacted why didn't the northerners have to free their slaves then?

The only two issues left on the table to fight for are States Rights and taxes. That goes back to what Mr. Cruz, my ninth grade World History Teacher, told me: "All wars are over who has the power, who wants the power, who controls the money, and who wants to control the money."

With that in mind we can look at some of the actions that President Lincoln took during the Civil War:

1. He suspended the Writ of Habeas Corpus more than President Jefferson Davis.[lxi]

2. He closed down northern newspapers that supported allowing the south to leave peacefully (even if they were abolitionist).[lxii]

3. He encouraged the governor of Indiana to not call the legislature into session so they wouldn't vote on supporting a negotiated peace with the south.[lxiii]

4. He had the Maryland Legislature arrested because it appeared they were going to vote on letting the south leave the union peacefully.[lxiv]

5. He engineered the western counties in Virginia to secede and become West Virginia (interesting logic, it's illegal for Virginia to secede from the Union but okay for West Virginia to secede from Virginia without Virginia having a say in the matter).[lxv]

6. He manipulated events so the south appeared to fire the first shot and start the Civil War (in fact Major Anderson, the Union Commander at Fort Moultrie, SC, disabled his cannons and evacuated his men and supplies to Fort Sumter. Then President Lincoln ordered a naval supply

convoy to aid Major Anderson (while he was promising to have the federal troops at Sumter evacuated).[lxvi]

Lott discusses the long-standing problem of Federal taxes on southern trade.

"Taxes were a problem for the south long before the War Between The States. In the early 1800s tariffs were needed to protect northern industry in its infancy. By 1828 they were no longer needed and the northerners were greedy. The results were the tariffs of 1828 and 1832. One incident almost caused a civil war. South Carolina had refused to pay those high taxes."[lxvii]

It seems ironic that instead of slavery being the cause of the civil war, keeping the institution of slavery may have been Lincoln's hidden goal to stay in power.

I've sold books at four Sons of Confederate Veterans Reunions and spoke at several camp meetings. I've had many members tell me they believe the fact that construction started on Fort Sumter in 1829 and that by 1861 it was still unfinished, and several northern forts had been designed, funded, and built while it was incomplete is an example of how the North would do anything to control the South. To them this neglect of southern infrastructure was indicative of how the Union spent southern tax revenue and had become dependent on it to balance the federal budget.

In searching for a possible reason for such a delay I contacted Ranger Antoine Fletcher, Park Ranger at Fort Sumter/Fort Moultrie.[lxviii]

"You have to realize that when construction was started in 1829 they did not have the technology we have today. They used sailing ships to transport 60,000 tons of bedrock and 10,000 tons of granite from New England to the Charleston Harbor. Fort Sumter was built on a sandbar and built up to provide the foundation for the fort. Between technology, or lack of, and funding problems only ninety percent of the Fort was completed by April 1861."

Ranger Fletcher referred me to the internet link for a pamphlet: "Fort Sumter, Official Handbook." In reviewing that I found a book titled: "Fort Sumter: Anvil of War." The author, Frank Barnes, went into more detail.

"Fort Sumter was one of a series of coastal fortifications built after the War of 1812. . .

Plans for Fort Sumter were drawn up in 1827 and adopted on December 5, 1828. . . In the course of that winter Lt Henry Brewerton, Army Corps of Engineers, assumed charge of the project and commenced active operations. But progress was slow, and as late as 1834 the new fort was no more than a hollow pentagonal rock "mole" two feet above low water and open at one side to permit supply ships to pass to the interior. . .

Operations were suspended late in the autumn of 1834 when ownership of the site came into question. . . It was November 1841 before the Federal government received clear title to the 125 acres of "harbor" land.

Local brickyard capacities were small and millions of bricks were required. . .

By 1860 Fort Sumter outwardly possessed a formidable appearance. . . Outward appearances, however, were deceiving. Unruffled decades of peace had induced glacial slowness and indifference in Washington. The fort was far from being completed and according to U.S. Army Surgeon Samuel W. Crawford who came to know the place well, "in no condition for defense."

By December 1860, time as well as money had run out, and the fort was about to take on a political significance far beyond the military function it was originally intended to serve."[lxix]

Whether or not the South had a legitimate reason for believing they were being short-changed, the perception could be that they were not getting their money's worth.

My Take:

It appears that President Lincoln had other reasons for fighting. That he wanted to pick a fight with the South rather than have a peaceful, negotiated settlement of the issues at hand.

The logic then, as now, seems to be: "If you don't agree with me you must be evil." How can we have a meaningful dialogue if we don't listen?

Seven - Didn't the Southern States just want to control the Union?

The few people who asked this question seemed to believe the South had control of the federal government. They pointed to two, of what they considered facts from the history they were taught in school. First, that most of the Presidents prior to the Civil War came from the South. And second they pointed to the 3/5 clause of the U.S. Constitution as proof that the South was able to get more representation in the House of Representatives because each slave was added to the census and the South was able to increase the number of Congressmen assigned to their state and therefore it's power in the federal government.

I did not have to ask a Southerner for the answer to the first point. Lincoln was the sixteenth President. Listed below are the Presidents from Washington to Lincoln and the states they came from.

Washington –Virginia	Tyler – Virginia (supported
Adams- Massachusetts	States Rights but favored
Jefferson-Virginia	Federal growth)
Madison-Virginia	Polk-Tennessee
Monroe-Virginia	Taylor-Born in Virginia, elected
Adams-Massachusetts	from Kentucky
Jackson-Tennessee	Fillmore-New York
Van Buren-New York	Pierce-New Hampshire
Harrison-Ohio	Buchanan-Pennsylvania
	Lincoln-Illinois

From the list above we see that six of the first fifteen Presidents were from Virginia or another southern state, and none were from

Virginia or the South after President Taylor. So at the beginning of the Civil War the South's "control" of the North was negligible.

Regarding the Northerner's second point Christopher Dickey makes this comment:

> "According to the original U.S. Constitution, slaves, who had no rights whatsoever as citizens, would be counted as three-fifths of a person for the census that determined a state's representation in Congress. This constitutional right—for such it was—was not one the slave-holding states were willing to give up, because they feared if they lost their disproportionate power in Washington, eventually their "right" to own other human beings to clear their land, grow their crops, and make their fortunes for them would be challenged."[lxx]

I found Lott's response to Dickey's statement in his manuscript.

> "There was a compromise between the small and large states, by which equality was secured to all the states in the senate, There was another compromise finally carried under threats from the south, on the motion of a New England member, by which the slave states were allowed Representatives according to the whole number of free persons, and three-fifths of all other persons," thus securing political power on account of their slaves, in consideration that direct taxes should be apportioned in the same way."[lxxi]

Seabrook had comments on this issue also:

> "Control of the Union" was the objective of the North, not the South. During the many congressional squabbles between South and North that preceded Lincoln's War, the South was only seeking to rebalance the scales of power, which had swung over to the Northern side after decades of levying tyrannical policies on Dixie. As for the Three-Fifths Clause, it was an invention of Northerners, not Southerners!"[lxxii]

34

To him this was proof of the South's not wanting to control the Union from the beginning of our country. Now let's see what he has to say about the South wanting to control the Union in 1861.

"More proof that the Southern states had no interest in "controlling the Union" is the fact that they seceded from it legally and peacefully; or at least attempted to do so, until they were halted by Lincoln's unwarranted military assault on their new constitutionally formed republic, the Confederate States of America (named after the original name for the United States of America). As Southern hero confederate President Jefferson Davis said at the time: "In independence we seek no conquest, no aggrandizement, no cession of any kind from the states with which we have lately confederated. All we ask is to be let alone."[lxxiii]

For more on these topics, see Seabrook's books Confederacy 101: Amazing Facts You Never Knew About America's Oldest Political Tradition; The Constitution of the Confederate States of America Explained; and The Articles of Confederation Explained."

My Take:

It appears to me that while some might contend the South was trying to control the federal government, Southerners can make a case for their point of view.

This section shows that the south was not interested in controlling the north. Every comment regarding power was complaining about northern control of the southern economy.

Eight - Didn't the CSA VP Believe that Slavery was the Cause of the Civil War?

Seabrook addresses this issue quite well in four clear quotes.

1. "In Stephens' infamous "Cornerstone Speech" (given March 21, 1861, at Savannah, Georgia), it is held that he made the statement that the "cornerstone [of the Constitution of the Southern Confederacy] rests upon the great truth, that the negro is not equal to the white man; that slavery . . . is his natural and normal condition." Were these Stephens' original words? Not according to the speaker himself. Not only was his speech given extemporaneous, but the version of it that has come down to us today is not a literal translation, but a loose "interpretation" of what he said by journalists in the audience. This is why Stephens later repeatedly asserted that his words had been misinterpreted and thus misunderstood."[lxxiv]

It would appear that like the game I used to play as a child where we would go around the room whispering a message from one person to another. The end result was something totally different from what we started with.

2. "However, even if we take the above quote literally, it is far from what pro-North historians claim it to be. It turns out that it was the North which believed that "slavery is the cornerstone of American society," for Stephens was merely citing the speech of a Yankee judge, Associate Justice of the Peace of the Supreme Court, Henry Baldwin of Connecticut, who, 28 years earlier (in 1833) said: "Slavery is the cornerstone of the [U.S.] Constitution. The foundations of

36

the Government are laid and rest on the rights of property in slaves, and the whole structure must fall by disturbing the cornerstone."[lxxv]

This would negate the claim that Mr. Stephens was stating that "slavery is the cornerstone of American society,"

3. "In the end, as Richard M. Johnson noted in 1884, all Stephens did during his speech was accurately point out the fact that "on the subject of slavery there was no essential change in the new [Southern Confederate] Constitution from the old [U.S. Constitution]."[lxxvi]

4. "The final nail in the coffin of this particular Yankee fairy tale is the fact that Stephens was known far and wide as a "true friend of the black man," an epithet that was never once applied to Lincoln while he was alive, and for obvious reasons: this was the same man who referred to blacks as "niggers," detested the abolition movement, implemented extreme racist military policies, supported the 1861 Corwin Amendment (which would have allowed slavery to continue in perpetuity if the Southern states agreed to return to the Union), was a lifelong member of the anti-black organization the American Colonization Society, who barred African-Americans from the White House, who blocked black suffrage and black citizenship, and who used slave labor to finish the Capital dome in Washington, D.C. For additional information on Stephens, see my books The Alexander H. Stephens Reader and The Quotable Alexander H. Stephens."[lxxvii]

My Take:

From Seabrook's comments it seems clear that there was not a written copy of Mr. Stephen's speech. Therefore reporters, or anyone in the decades since, could have misinterpreted his comments. More importantly it appears that Stephens was just stating what was legal in 1861. He was not advocating slavery. In fact he was party to the drafting of the Confederate Constitution which gave each state the right to choose to be a slave or Free State, and the drafters of the Confederate Constitution purposely chose not to allow the reactivation of the Atlantic Slave Trade in the Confederate States of America.

Nine - How has History Led Us to Where We are Today?

Recent current events in Ferguson, Baltimore and Charleston, prompted me to contact Traywick, and Seabrook for their response to these additional questions:

1. Is the Confederate Battle Flag a symbol of hatred and racism?

2. All Confederate monuments need to be taken down.

3. The rise of the KKK is proof that the South hasn't learned its lesson from the original conflict.

Seabrook has a few interesting points that many people, even some Southerners, do not realize.

> "The Confederate Battle Flag was not the emblem of the national government of the Confederate States of America. It was the official flag of the Confederate military — which had nothing to do with politics or social institutions. It was only used by Rebel army and navy officers and their soldiers. What does this usage have to do with either slavery or racism? Even if it had been the official national flag, the C.S.A. was not fighting over slavery. It was fighting for constitutional freedom and to protect the lives, homes, and land of its citizens against an aggressive and unwanted intruder."[lxxviii]

That covers his view on the Confederate Battle Flag. He now brings up an aspect of North and South relations that I'd never thought of.

What the North does not understand, or understands but refuses to honor, is that Southerners have lived under two national flags: the U.S. Flag and the C.S. Flag. Both are important to us here in the South (though for different reasons). In a very real sense, this makes Southerners dual citizens of the United States. We are both Unionists (U.S.A.) and Confederates (C.S.A.), and so we have a double allegiance."[lxxix]

Once I thought about this I realized it is true. I've known many Southerners in my adult life. I would venture to say that all of them have been Patriots (to the original U.S. Constitution). They want to have the truth of the Civil War told. They are willing to listen to the northern view of what caused the conflict, but want their view to be heard also. Seabrook continues.

"This is the reality. The truth is that there have been far more racial crimes committed under the U.S. Flag than the C.S. Flag, and if the Left truly practiced what it preaches, it would ban the former not the latter. We could start with slavery, as just one example. Every American slave vessel to ever sail from the U.S. left from Northern ports aboard Northern slave vessels, that were designed by Northern engineers, constructed by Northern shipbuilders, fitted out by Northern riggers, piloted by Northern ship captains, manned by Northern crews, launched from Northern marine ports, funded by Northern businessmen, all which was supported by the vast majority of the anti-abolitionist Northern population. The number of Africans who were abused and who died on these voyages is beyond counting. But we never hear a word from Liberals about taking down the U.S. Flag, only the C.S. Flag."[lxxx]

This is an interesting point of view. He's not negating the South's involvement in slavery, just pointing out that the North was heavily involved. So why the furor? Why does the "Left" continue to push the idea that the conflict was about slavery and all Southerners were evil?

"But it's really not the flag they hate, is it? It's what it represents: the conservative, Christian, traditional South. For traditional Southerners the Confederate Battle Flag remains a powerful emblem of our history as a once proud, separate and sovereign country. This sentiment is not going to change now or in the future, and the sooner this is accepted by enemies of the South the better for everyone. For more on the Confederate Battle Flag, see my book Confederate Flag Facts."[lxxxi]

Seabrook continues with an interesting point of view:

"American Liberalism can only thrive if its constituents are made to feel unsatisfied about life in the U.S. Since, thanks to the Constitution, we live in one of the richest, and certainly one of the most egalitarian countries in the world, progressives must fabricate various issues to stir up this discontentment."[lxxxii]

I've witnessed the hatred coming from Fergusson and Baltimore. The news blamed the South before the facts were in. it seems the Liberals had their minds made up before the news feed reached the first commercial. Seabrook continues:

"Among these they have invented "the war against women," "the war between the rich and the poor," and "the war between selfish stone-hearted Conservatives and generous compassionate Liberals," just to name a few. Their favorite fake conflict, however, is "the war between the races."[lxxxiii]

The idea of Liberals controlling the media and conspiring against Conservatives has been around for a long time. It's like the concept has taken on a new life. Seabrook continues:

"Race baiting is not new to Liberals. They have been pulling out the race card for decades. One of the first Liberals to engage in the merchandising of bigotry was arch white racist Abraham Lincoln, who very intentionally invented an imaginary race war between southern whites and southern

41

blacks. Indeed, this was one of the purposes of his Emancipation Proclamation: to stir up racial animosity in Dixie in order to foment a region-wide "slave insurrection." As the document itself tacitly suggests, he and his administration hoped that this would tear the South apart, and in doing so, undermine southern society to the point where she would be easier to subdue."[lxxxiv]

Now Seabrook reflects back on Mr. Lincoln's actions.

"Unfortunately for the Great White Supremacist, not a single race riot occurred in the South during his war. The vast majority of Southern blacks remained loyal and on friendly terms with their owners both during and after the conflict, proving once again, if more proof is needed, that Southern "slavery" was not the cruel and racist institution the North has long claimed it to be. Though Lincoln died before he could see the disastrous fruits of his war on the Constitution and the American people, the liberal Yankee politicians who survived him were hell-bent on perpetuating his contrived "race war," even without a shred of evidence that such racism existed in the South."[lxxxv]

It appears that he has a point. In all my history courses I never heard of such a concept. But how did they begin?

"One of the first methods they utilized after Dishonest Abe's death was to send thousands of dyed-in-the-wool Yankee school teachers to the Southern states. Their purpose? To erode and ultimately destroy traditional Southern culture by "reeducating" Southern children in Northern ways and Northern history. Part of this deceptive and false curriculum was the teaching that the South was "bad" because it was "built on slavery," and that Southerners were "racist" because they kept slaves. Naturally these unwanted invading "educators" ignored the facts that slavery has been practiced world-wide by all races (and is therefore not an inherently racist institution), that American slavery began in the North, that it was not the

South but the North that had been constructed around slavery, and that America possessed thousands of black, brown, and red slave owners before the War."[lxxxvi]

It seems there are many issues that had been hidden from my education, and generations of others, that I'd never considered. I didn't think it was possible for other issues to come up. But Seabrook has more for our education.

"Without question the most powerful ploy that post-bellum Yankee liberals used to continue Lincoln's counterfeit race war was the creation of the Union League or Black Loyal League, as it was called. The alleged purpose of the Northern organization was to help dislocated Southern blacks find housing and jobs, who were typically tempted by U.S. government agents with the insincere offer of "forty acres and a mule. In reality, few if any of the North's promises ever panned out, including this one: the forthcoming mules were nonexistent and seized Southern land was given mainly to wealthy white Yankee industrialists.

Consequently, African-Americans received little help in integrating into postwar America, and an estimated 25 percent of Southern blacks died in the aftermath of the Emancipation Proclamation and Reconstruction."[lxxxvii]

I remember my college history courses covering "Carpetbaggers." They never mentioned more than they were Northerners who were making sacrifices to help the former slaves adjust to their new lives. It seems the Carpetbagger backstory is deeper than I ever imagined.

"The truth is that the League was merely a front to conceal the North's numerous anti-South activities, one of which was to inculcate Southern blacks with the notion that their white owners were vicious racists who had been using and abusing them for the past 250 years. Thus, with Dixie now weakened and in tatters, the Union League added bribery and intimidation to its campaign to turn the agricultural-religious south into an exact duplicate of the industrial atheistic north.

This treacherous Northernization process included paying blacks to stir up animosity against not only their former owners, but all Southern whites. When that Yankee plan failed, threats of violence were employed against African-Americans (mainly the illiterate) with predictable results: anti-white hate crimes committed by Southern blacks rose precipitously, fueling the development of anti-black sentiment across [the South.] This so-called "white racism," in turn, was used by the Grant Administration and the Northern press to inflame already existing anti-South prejudices in the Northeast, the fulfillment of part of Lincoln's nefarious "white dream" to divide and conquer America. (No mention was ever made that Grant himself was a racist slave owner who, during the War, said that he didn't care about abolition and would rather join the Confederacy than fight to end slavery.)"[lxxxviii]

So the stage was set, freed slaves who were primed to hate their former masters and whites in general, were portrayed as evil and not to be trusted.

"But the Yankees' phony race war was short-lived. With the end of "Reconstruction" in 1877, the removal of the last detested Union soldier from Dixie, and the return of former Confederate politicians to office, Southern race relations reverted to their original mutually respectful and affectionate state.

Just as throughout the antebellum period, the South once again became the least racist region of the country, a status it has retained to this day—despite ongoing attempts by the anti-South movement to portray it otherwise."[lxxxix]

Seabrook has made a few interesting points, I don't hear him saying that all southern whites were perfect or that all northern carpetbaggers were evil. What he is saying is that the true Southerner isn't the type of person the northern liberals would like us to believe in. It would be interesting, if a northern liberal would sit down and actually discuss the issues, to see what could be accomplished.

When I interviewed Winbush in July 2012, I asked why a black man would fight for the south. He smiled and said:

> "The Union soldiers ran roughshod over the common people, some of whom were trying to be neutral and maintain a living. The first thing the Union soldiers did when they overran a plantation was rape the slave women, when they ran out of them they would rape the 'missy girls' (young slave girls who hadn't reached puberty)." He paused and looked at me, "Now who would you fight for?"[xc]

During the war Union soldiers raped and pillaged throughout the south. Sherman aggressively destroyed everything in his path, whether it was needed to support the southern war effort or not.

After the war the Carpetbaggers came in and taught the freed slaves that they deserved to be taken care of by the government and their former owners were responsible for their plight. These are the same Southerners who a few months before had been treating their slaves like family.

The next response comes from Traywick:

> "There has been some controversy generated by the Confederate Battle Flag that was hoisted over Interstate 95 near Richmond. The arguments against it are the predictable ones, such as that it is "divisive;" it makes Richmond look like a "hick town" full of "ignorant people;" that we ought to be "looking ahead" instead of "looking back" at something we have "moved on" from; and that it will hurt "tourism" if we tell the Truth about our grandparents' fathers instead of selling them down the river to gawking tourists as scapegoats for all the social ills of this nation.

The unspoken assumption is that The War was fought over slavery, and the implications of this assumption are that if anyone disagrees with this point of view, they are either a "racist" or an "ignorant redneck" stuck in the past. I thought we had put away all those racial stereotypes."[xci]

In a sense Dylan Roof committed his horrible crime against everyone, not only against members of the Emmanuel African-American Episcopal Church in Charleston, but everyone of any race, culture, or creed who has a close relationship with our Lord Jesus Christ. The forgiveness shown by the believers of that church is a tribute to their faith.

The next issue that has come up recently is the call to tear down Confederate Monuments. As usual the American public has a knee-jerk reaction to almost every horrible catastrophe. Let's see what Seabrook has to say:

"As mentioned, Southerners are dual citizens of the U.S. The Southern states once formed their own independent republic, and so we have a different history, with different symbols, different heroes, different stories, different legends, different memories, than the North.

Why can this fact not be respected? It is because the traditional South is largely Christian, constitutionalist, and conservative, things that are detested by many Liberals and nearly all socialists, Marxists, communists, and anti-Southerners."[xcii]

I always remember my mother telling me that if you lose your temper in an argument it usually means that you don't have your facts straight, and you resort to anger to prove your point. It's sad to see people who riot in their own cities and destroy their own neighborhoods to get back at their "enemy." Or anti-abortion activists who bomb an abortion clinic to get their point across.

To that end the knee-jerk reaction of removing the Confederate Battle Flag and Confederate Monuments from public display seems to be over-reacting. Seabrook continues.

"We say what does it matter if we have a statue of our greatest leader, President Jefferson Davis, in front of our city hall? Our enemies reply: "Because Davis was a traitor to the U.S. and a racist who owned slaves." To this we say both secession and slavery were legal at the time. As for the charge of racism, Davis adopted an orphaned black boy (named Jim Limber) during the War, something that white racists simply do not do."[xciii]

Seabrook is one Southerner who's revealed information the Liberals would rather not have in the education system. It appears that the "Liberals" want us to believe everything about the conflict was one-hundred-eighty degrees from reality.

"Let us keep in mind that it was Lincoln, not Davis, who repeatedly and publicly called blacks an "inferior race," even referring to them as "niggers" on occasion. And it was Lincoln who, in his Inaugural Address, promised not to interfere with slavery and who was ready to sign the Corwin Amendment (a bill that would have allowed slavery to continue in perpetuity if the Southern states agreed to return to the Union). And it was Lincoln who committed treason when he violated the U.S. Constitution by initiating war without congressional approval."[xciv]

If we read today's headlines it appears as if history is repeating itself. Could this be a reason for feeding us the lies? I remember the old adage: "Those who chose to ignore history are bound to repeat it."

"Using the twisted, intolerant logic of the Liberal Yankee, is it not time to remove all of the statues of Lincoln, erase his face from our money, license plates, and Mount Rushmore, and tear down his grotesque Pagan monument in Washington, D.C.? We embrace the Constitution and the

First Amendment, and so do not wish to censor our enemies the way they do us. However, if they were not hypocrites this is exactly what they would do."[xcv]

I haven't heard a single Southerner ask, insist, or even mention the idea that Lincoln should be removed from his place in history. All I hear them saying is let us have our history. "You can believe what you want to believe and all we ask is for you to let us believe what we believe."

Along these lines Seabrook states:

"Let us be clear. The Southern Confederate States of America was a reality from 1861 to 1865, and countless hundreds of thousands of Southerners died trying to defend it. No amount of persecution, no prohibition, no threats, no law, no matter how many are passed, will ever obliterate these facts.

The C.S.A. is part and parcel of American history, and the people who participated in it—courageous Southern men and women who simply acted on their constitutional rights at the time—as well as their descendants should be recognized, respected, and honored. Taking away our memorials will never change that.

We will never allow our Confederate forbears to be forgotten. We will never stop honoring them. We will never stop fighting for the Southern Cause. We will never stop celebrating our history."[xcvi]

Traywick also comes up with some interesting angles to the issues at hand:

"Is the past that is reconstructed by historians a revival or a "new show"? Paul A. Cohen asks this question in his book History in Three Keys: The Boxers as Event, Experience, and Myth (New York: Columbia UP, 1997). He answers that the history created by historians is fundamentally different from the history made by the people of the times.

The professional historian's objective is to understand the past and then explain it as "event," whereas those who made the history explain it as "experience." The historian tries to look at the past objectively, whereas the people who made the history tend to look at it subjectively, and in a fashion that is psychologically tolerable to themselves. If such subjectivity becomes validated by communal consensus, then myths can be created in place of intellectual truth. "Myth" is the third way of can an objective historian be a purveyor of myth? However committed he may be to the objective truth, he remains a product of his own culture, and he is subjected in varying degrees to its cultural imperatives, its "world view." How much cultural subjectivity goes into a historian's selection of historical matter to be examined or theses to be argued? How much pressure are professional historians under to be admitted to a course of study, to hold tenure, to gain grants, and to stay in good professional and financial graces with the powers that dispense these things?"[xcvii]

That was a long answer but I felt it was important for Traywick to explain his point of view. He continues with his commentary.

"It should come as no surprise to see that the most powerful nation in history has at its disposal the most powerful and extensive means for disseminating its own version of history. From the history books used in grammar schools, high schools and colleges, to television "docu-dramas", Hollywood romantics, National Park Service presentations, and the lurid sensationalism of the media, America has just as much incentive to tell its own story as "creatively" as anyone – and it has its own stable of "Court Historians" groomed to tell it."[xcviii]

It's as if the northern point-of-view is the only one that matters, the only one that deserves to be heard.

"The North's war against Southern secession is a glaring example. The story trumpeted from the heights is that the

North fought to free the slaves and the South fought to keep them. End of story. Any questions?

Well, yes. Something doesn't compute, here. If the North was waging a war against slavery, why didn't she wage war on New York and Boston, the two largest African slave-trading ports in the world at the time of Lincoln's election? Or on New England cotton mills and their profits from slave-picked cotton? Or on northern iron foundries that forged the shackles and chains? Or on New England rum distilleries that made rum from slave-harvested sugar cane to use for barter on the African coast? Or on New England shipyards that built the slave ships?

Or on the African slave-catchers, such as the Kingdom of Dahomey, the largest exporters of African slaves in the world for five hundred years? And why did Lincoln's Emancipation Proclamation say that slavery was alright as long as one was loyal to his government?"[xcix]

Next he makes his point that Northerners don't want to accept. Because if they do then the issue they cite as the cause of the conflict doesn't make sense. But here he makes a point that states the Southern point-of-view quite well.

"Why? Because the "Irrepressible Conflict" was not waged over slavery, as Senator Seward would have it. The "Irrepressible Conflict" was between a Northern industrial economy that wanted to burst the constraints of a federative Constitution and a Southern agrarian economy that didn't. The peaceful secession of the South at the election of a strictly sectional Northern party in 1860 should have resolved the situation, but with the South out of the Union, the North would have lost its source of cotton for its mills, its largest source of tariff revenues, its largest market for its manufactured goods, and control of the mouth of the Mississippi. The North's nascent industrial economy would wither on the vine, so – at the behest of the Northern industrialists, railroad magnates, and financiers who got him elected – Lincoln provoked the South into firing the first shot, got the war he wanted, marched his armies across the South, and drove the Southern States back into the Union at the point of the bayonet. Reconstruction then destroyed the federative nature of the Constitution, centralized power into the Federal Government, and put it in the hands of the industrial North.

With the Northern victory, the States – who created the Federal Government - are no longer the final arbiters of the limits of its power. The Supreme Court is. But the Supreme Court is part of the Federal Government. Therefore the Federal Government is the final arbiter of the limits of its own power, and that is the very definition of despotism. However, this doesn't look too good in a fourth grade history book or on a Ken Burns TV show, so it must all be buried under a mountain of slavery and emancipation. This is the American Myth, validated by communal consensus and eternally re-enforced by ham-fisted morality plays such as the recent "Sesquicentennial of the Civil War and Emancipation," while the Confederacy has been made the convenient scapegoat for all the racial ills in America.

But those who bash the Confederacy and vandalize her monuments are merely beating a horse that has been dead for a hundred and fifty years. As Edmund Burke warned, you are gibbeting the carcass while your house is the haunt of robbers."[c]

The last question that I gave my southern friends is: Was the rise of the KKK is proof that the South hasn't learned its lesson from the original conflict.

"After the war southern veterans (black and white) were being mistreated, that inspired General Nathan Bedford Forrest, about a year after it was formed, to accept the position of Grand Wizard of the Ku Klux Klan. In the beginning it was a benevolent organization to provide for the welfare of the men who had supported the south. They wore bed sheets to disguise themselves from the Northerners who were oppressing them. When evil influences started to take over the Klan, he tried to disband it. Eventually it was resurrected into that evil organization and the General is blamed for all the evil that it has accomplished."[ci]

Seabrook comes up with several points:

"This question betrays a complete ignorance of both Southern history and American history! What does the Ku Klux Klan have to do with the South, and why are the two so integrally connected in the public mind?

Let's examine this for those who are uninformed on the matter. There have been two KKKs in American history. The first I call the "Civil War KKK." The second, the "Modern KKK." The Civil War KKK lasted only from December 1865 to early 1869, and was an anti-Yankee organization, or more specifically, an anti-carpetbag organization; a social aid and welfare society whose main purpose was to protect the widowed, orphaned, and dis-possessed, while helping maintain law and order during so-called "Reconstruction." Not only did the Southern Civil War KKK have thousands of black members, there was an all-black KKK chapter in Nashville at one time."[cii]

An all-black KKK chapter? The Liberals never mention that? It's almost as if they erase southern history they don't agree with it will make the northern history more right.

"The Modern KKK, created after 1900, has no connection whatsoever to the Civil War KKK. The only thing they share in common is their name. Indeed, they are so completely dissimilar in every way that if the modern KKK hadn't borrowed the name of the original KKK, no educated individual today would even make any connection between the two.

In my opinion the present day rise of the KKK can be attributed, in large part, to the race-baiting, race merchants of the current administration and its socialistic followers and sycophants. I've been saying for decades, and will continue to say that only racists see racism in everything and everyone, and only racists judge people by the color of their skin. Non-racists, like most traditional Southerners, could care less about skin color and instead judge others by their character."[ciii]

Which area of the U.S. is more racist? Where does the problem lie? Seabrook has a few interesting points.

"To any objective person it's obvious that the North is far more racist than the South; and by this I mean not just white racism, but also black and brown racism. This is because racism, among all colors, grows most virulently where liberalism is most strongly established, and in America this is primarily in the Northeast. All the racial hatred toward white Southerners is flowing from the north southward, not just from blacks, but from Northern whites as well. Isn't that interesting? These are the same people calling our flag a "symbol of hate"!

Actually, you'll see very little hatred of any kind here in Dixie, because we're more accepting of others, and always have been. Early writers, tourists, and foreign visitors to the U.S. made hundreds of remarks about this striking difference between the South and North. Highly educated men, like French diplomat Alexis de Tocqueville, for example, was appalled by the entrenched white racism in the North, and pleasantly surprised by the racial tolerance among whites in the South."[civ]

Considering the Charleston shooting, some might disagree. But to paint an entire culture as evil because of one troubled individual seems ludicrous. He continues.

"This is why the recent resurgence in the KKK is taking place most rapidly outside the South. In fact, since the 1920s, there have always been more KKK chapters and more racial-based hate crimes in the North than in the South. The anti-South movement doesn't want you to know this, so it has rewritten history to make it appear as if the South is the racist culprit, not the North. But truth cannot be destroyed by editing it or suppressing it. So let's stop associating the South with white racism and the KKK. It's unfair, inaccurate, and unhistorical."[cv]

Lenzini has similar feelings/beliefs on the KKK as Seabrook. I include them because he brings up a few interesting angles to our discussion.

"Do NOT be confused... The Confederate Battle Flag IS NOT the official flag of the KKK. Television, history books, the media, the school systems, etc. abound in false-hoods and inaccuracies concerning the Confederate States of America Battle flag. Mainly, that the Confederate Battle Flag is a symbol that represents slavery, terror, crime and that it represents the KKK.

BUT, this is far from the truth. Of all KKK meetings, actual photographs/films from past to present, KKK cable access talk shows, etc. all PROUDLY boast as being an AMERICAN society. NOT a Southern or Confederate society!!!!! But AMERICAN!!!"[cvi]

It appears that the Liberals are accusing southern culture of supporting the KKK when the KKK doesn't claim southern heritage.

"Along with that, over 95 percent of the flags they fly are of the United States of America's "Stars and Stripes" flag!!!! As well, in the height of the KKK movement, the largest segment was from the north in the 1920's. And the Grand Dragon was from the Federal stronghold of Indiana. A man

54

by the name of David Stevenson. There were over 6 million members at this time!!!! This is plain and simple.

Don't believe it??? Then take a look at the photos below (which date from turn of century to present) and see for yourself!!!! A picture is worth a hundred thousand words in this case..."[cvii]

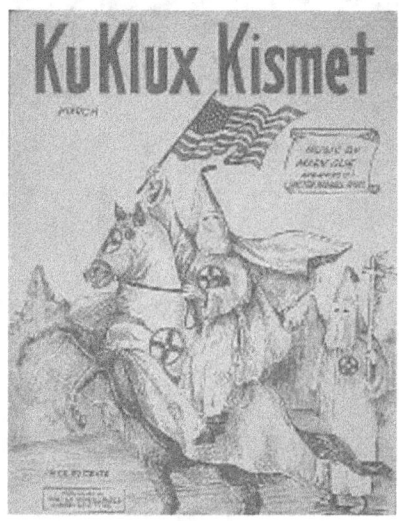

"So, as you can plainly see, heritage groups such as the SCV and descendants of the Confederacy have been "painted" in a negative light due to the media, etc. And the Confederate Battle Flag literally DOESN"T EVEN ENTER THE PICTURE!!!!!

As a matter of fact, heritage groups such as the SCV - Sons Of Confederate Veterans, battle daily the damage done to a proud nation by these hate groups."[cviii]

It shouldn't be a surprise to anyone that the Jim Crow laws came about, that the evil KKK became as powerful as it did. In science we're taught that for every action there's an equal and opposite reaction. Here we see the same principal in southern society.

I'm repeating a previous statement by Seabrook to emphasize the point that many people seem to ignore, when he asks: Why is the Old South portrayed as a "racist region"?

"American Liberalism can only thrive if its constituents are made to feel unsatisfied about life in the U.S.. Since, thanks to the Constitution, we live in one of the richest, and certainly one of the most egalitarian countries in the world, progressives must fabricate various issues to stir up this discontentment.

Among these they have invented "the war against women," "the war between the rich and the poor," and "the war between selfish stone-hearted Conservatives and generous compassionate Liberals," just to name a few. Their favorite fake conflict, however, is "the war between the races."[cix]

I'm sure many Liberals will disagree. After all if they were to agree they would have to disavow their core beliefs.

"Race baiting is not new to Liberals. They have been pulling out the race card for decades. One of the first Liberals to engage in the merchandising of bigotry was arch white racist Abraham Lincoln, who very intentionally invented an imaginary race war between Southern whites and Southern blacks. Indeed, this was one of the purposes of his Emancipation Proclamation: to stir up racial animosity in Dixie in order to foment a region-wide "slave insurrection." As the document itself tacitly suggests, he and his administration hoped that this would tear the South apart, and in doing so, undermine Southern society to the point where she would be easier to subdue."[cx]

For some Liberals who have stayed with our discussion this may be a little harsh. But if we're to be fair to the South we need to let the Southerners have their say in the matter.

"Unfortunately for the Great White Supremacist, not a single race riot occurred in the South during his war. The vast majority of Southern blacks remained loyal and on friendly terms with their owners both during and after the conflict, proving once again, if more proof is needed, that Southern "slavery" was not the cruel and racist institution the North has long claimed it to be.

Though Lincoln died before he could see the disastrous fruits of his war on the Constitution and the American people, the liberal Yankee politicians who survived him were hell-bent on perpetuating his contrived "race war," even without a shred of evidence that such racism existed in the South."[cxi]

I can hear some of my Liberal friends questioning how this could be accomplished. I'm repeating a comment from Seabrook to emphasize his point also.

"One of the first methods they utilized after Dishonest Abe's death was to send thousands of dyed-in-the-wool Yankee school teachers to the Southern states. Their purpose? To erode and ultimately destroy traditional Southern culture by "reeducating" Southern children in Northern ways and Northern history. Part of this deceptive and false curriculum was the teaching that the South was "bad" because it was "built on slavery," and that

Southerners were "racist" because they kept slaves. Naturally these unwanted invading "educators" ignored the facts that slavery has been practiced worldwide by all races (and is therefore not an inherently racist institution), that American slavery began in the North, that it was not the South but the North that had been constructed around slavery, and that America possessed thousands of black, brown, and red slave owners before the War."[cxii]

That's one aspect of the slavery question that many Liberal educators leave out. That the white race wasn't the only participant in slavery. I wonder if we could conduct a DNA test on some of the black and red slave owners if we would find that some of the most vehement anti-southern blacks actually have a fair percentage of "slave owner" blood in their veins. Seabrook continues.

"Consequently, African-Americans received little help in integrating into postwar America, and an estimated 25 percent of Southern blacks died in the aftermath of the Emancipation Proclamation and Reconstruction."[cxiii]

My Take:

I wonder where the Liberals will place the blame for that 25 percent. Or do Black Lives from the past Matter?

It appears that Southern blacks have been getting it from both sides.

Northerners were selling them the concept of: "The whites owe you, they did you wrong."

Many Southerners were reacting with, that's not fair, and we don't deserve this.

This is a generalization, but there is a lot of truth to the statement. Over the past century-and-a-half with both sides not listening to the other, and responding with an answer before their "opponent" finishes their thought. The end result has been race riots, mistrust of law enforcement, and the "system."

Conclusion

From everything I've heard and read throughout this exercise it is that both Northerners and Southerners bear responsibility for American Slavery. Logic says the northern slave-traders would not have been in business if the Southern slave-owner hadn't been a willing customer, so both were responsible.

As we discussed earlier, northerners freed their slaves in the early 1800s. In my opinion, they acted like a recovered alcoholic who had been given a field sobriety test, and under the old standard passed. Then after he's been sober for a while condemns his brother for failing a field sobriety test under a new and stricter standard. To me it appears the Abolitionists were proud that they were now righteous. Some may say it's a simplistic way of looking at it, but what would the outcome have been if the Abolitionists hadn't insisted the Southerners meet a standard they hadn't and couldn't have met and then had pushed for southern slavery to be phased out?

England's empire and economy was much larger than the United States' at the time. They were able to eliminate slavery by compensating slave owners.[cxiv] It's possible that if such a plan had been negotiated that the United States wouldn't be paired with Haiti as the only two countries who eliminated slavery through violence.

That brings up the question, "If the institution of slavery wasn't the main cause of the Civil War what was?

We can consider the issue of "States Rights." This would apply Traywick's formula from an earlier chapter. Consider: How is the American Revolution similar to the Civil War?

1. England refused to let the American Colonies become independent.

2. The Union refused to let the Southern States secede.

3. England ran roughshod over the common people, some of whom were trying to be neutral and just maintain a living.

4. Is there any doubt that General Sherman's march to the sea filled that aspect of the analogy?

Would Northerners agree that the Founding Fathers were wrong in rebelling against England? If not would they consider letting Southerners have the point that their ancestors had a legal right to secede?

Then we have everyone in-between who might have been reasonable if they weren't boxed into a corner and forced to choose (Robert E. Lee is the most prominent Southerner that comes to mind). Would it have been possible for the United States of America to phase out slavery in a similar manner to England?

But this doesn't answer the question. Why? Why were Haiti and the USA the only societies who had to eliminate slavery with violence?

I recall Jesus' words:

> "And why do you look at the speck in your brother's eye, but do not consider the plank in your own eye?"[cxv]

Abolitionists had slavery in their culture's past. They claimed the moral high ground and felt it was necessary to force others to believe the way they did. Over the decades since Pennsylvania and other North Atlantic states phased out slavery they were insisting that Southerners immediately free their slaves with no payment for the economic upheaval such an act would cause. This is the society that wanted to free the slaves but not treat them as equals. At best they wanted to send them all back to Africa, regardless of where they had been born.[cxvi]

Then we have some Southerners, Robert E. Lee was the most prominent that comes to mind, who freed slaves that were in their control. Unfortunately people like him, and others who were more in the middle of the political spectrum, were forced to choose between their homeland and the people they loved and people who had sworn to eliminate them.

Both Yankees and Rebels had strong Christians on their side. Both sets of Christians were fighting for their God and their country. Then as now, people seem to feel that since "I am righteous I have a right to force my belief on others." And that anyone who doesn't believe the way they do must be unrighteous.

It sounds simplistic, but when we strip away all the historical events, we have both sides believing the other has committed unpardonable sins against them and must pay.

The only explanation I can give someone is for them to list each of their righteous deeds on one piece of paper. Then pile all those righteous deeds in one stack. I could say to myself, "Hey, I'm not so bad am I?" Especially when I compare myself to that evil Adolf Hitler, "I must be pretty good, after all look at how small his pile is." Now let's compare myself to God's righteousness. His stack must go to the sun if not out to the planet Pluto and beyond. So if I can't forgive my fellow man, how can I expect God to forgive me? By the same token, couldn't we apply that analogy to the 1860s?

When I started this journey and began to ask questions I had no idea where it would end up. Then it came to me. What is the one emotion that pervades the issue? From the beginning of American Slavery, to the recent Church shooting in Charleston?

Hatred and un-forgiveness seem to cover everything. You don't have one without the other. Personally I've had to deal with un-forgiveness. My ex-wife claimed she had forgiven me for the wrongs I'd done while we were married. However, from what my grown children have told me she never missed a day when she didn't complain about how evil a man I was. Here she was claiming The Lord's forgiveness and she couldn't forgive me.

With that in mind what if, in the decades prior to the Civil War, both sides had focused on their relationship to Almighty God? Would they might have been more willing to listen to their adversary and could we have had a different course of history?

I wish this chapter was the conclusion, that people of all races and creeds could live in peace and harmony. We need to listen to what our opponent has to say, not think of our response before they finish their initial statement.

Appendix A – Federalist Papers

FEDERALIST No. 39

The Conformity of the Plan to Republican Principles
For the Independent Journal.

James Madison

To the People of the State of New York:

THE last paper having concluded the observations which were meant to introduce a candid survey of the plan of government reported by the convention, we now proceed to the execution of that part of our undertaking. The first question that offers itself is, whether the general form and aspect of the government be strictly republican. It is evident that no other form would be reconcilable with the genius of the people of America; with the fundamental principles of the Revolution; or with that honorable determination which animates every votary of freedom, to rest all our political experiments on the capacity of mankind for self-government. If the plan of the convention, therefore, be found to depart from the republican character, its advocates must abandon it as no longer defensible.

What, then, are the distinctive characters of the republican form? Were an answer to this question to be sought, not by recurring to principles, but in the application of the term by political writers, to the constitution of different States, no satisfactory one would ever be found. Holland, in which no particle of the supreme authority is derived from the people, has passed almost universally under the denomination of a republic. The same title has been bestowed on Venice, where absolute power over the great body of the people is exercised, in the most absolute manner, by a small body of hereditary nobles. Poland, which is a mixture of aristocracy and of monarchy in their worst forms, has been dignified with the same appellation. The government of England, which has one republican branch only, combined with an hereditary aristocracy and monarchy, has, with equal impropriety, been frequently placed on the list of republics. These examples, which are nearly as dissimilar to each other as to a genuine republic, show the extreme inaccuracy with which the term has been used in political disquisitions.

If we resort for a criterion to the different principles on which different forms of government are established, we may define a republic to be, or at least may bestow that name on, a government which derives all its powers directly or indirectly from the great body of the people, and is administered by persons holding their offices during pleasure, for a limited period, or during good behavior. It is ESSENTIAL to such a government that it be derived from the great body of the society, not from an inconsiderable proportion, or a favored class of it; otherwise a handful of tyrannical nobles, exercising their oppressions by a delegation of their powers, might aspire to the rank of republicans, and claim for their government the honorable title of republic. It is SUFFICIENT for such a government that the persons administering it be appointed, either directly or indirectly, by the people; and that they hold their appointments by either of the tenures just specified; otherwise every government in the United States, as well as every other popular government that has been or can be well organized or well executed, would be degraded from the republican character. According to the constitution of every State in the Union, some or other of the officers of government are appointed indirectly only by the people. According to most of them, the chief magistrate himself is so appointed. And according to one, this mode of appointment is extended to one of the co-ordinate branches of the legislature. According to all the constitutions, also, the tenure of the highest offices is extended to a definite period, and in many instances, both within the legislative and executive departments, to a period of years. According to the provisions of most of the constitutions, again, as well as according to the most respectable and received opinions on the subject, the members of the judiciary department are to retain their offices by the firm tenure of good behavior.

On comparing the Constitution planned by the convention with the standard here fixed, we perceive at once that it is, in the most rigid sense, conformable to it. The House of Representatives, like that of one branch at least of all the State legislatures, is elected immediately by the great body of the people. The Senate, like the present Congress, and the Senate of Maryland, derives its appointment indirectly from the people. The President is indirectly derived from the choice of the people, according to the example in most of the States. Even the judges, with all other officers of the Union, will, as in the several States, be the choice, though a remote choice, of the people themselves, the duration of the appointments is equally conformable to the republican standard, and to the model of State constitutions The House of Representatives is periodically elective, as in all the States; and for the period of two years, as in the State of South Carolina. The Senate is elective, for the period of six years; which is but one year more than the period of the Senate of Maryland, and but two more than that of the Senates of New York and Virginia. The President is to continue in office for the period of four years; as in New York and Delaware, the chief magistrate is elected for three years, and in South Carolina for two years. In the other States the election is annual. In several of the States, however, no constitutional provision is made for the impeachment of the chief magistrate. And in Delaware and Virginia he is not impeachable till out of office. The President of the United States is impeachable at any time during his continuance in office. The tenure by which the judges are to hold their places, is, as it unquestionably ought to be, that of good behavior. The tenure of the ministerial offices generally, will be a subject of legal regulation, conformably to the reason of the case and the example of the State constitutions.

Could any further proof be required of the republican complexion of this system, the most decisive one might be found in its absolute prohibition of titles of nobility, both under the federal and the State governments; and in its express guaranty of the republican form to each of the latter.

"But it was not sufficient," say the adversaries of the proposed Constitution, "for the convention to adhere to the republican form. They ought, with equal care, to have preserved the FEDERAL form, which regards the Union as a CONFEDERACY of sovereign states; instead of which, they have framed a NATIONAL government, which regards the Union as a CONSOLIDATION of the States." And it is asked by what authority this bold and radical innovation was undertaken? The handle which has been made of this objection requires that it should be examined with some precision.

Without inquiring into the accuracy of the distinction on which the objection is founded, it will be necessary to a just estimate of its force, first, to ascertain the real character of the government in question; secondly, to inquire how far the convention were authorized to propose such a government; and thirdly, how far the duty they owed to their country could supply any defect of regular authority.

First. In order to ascertain the real character of the government, it may be considered in relation to the foundation on which it is to be established; to the sources from which its ordinary powers are to be drawn; to the operation of those powers; to the extent of them; and to the authority by which future changes in the government are to be introduced.

On examining the first relation, it appears, on one hand, that the Constitution is to be founded on the assent and ratification of the people of America, given by deputies elected for the special purpose; but, on the other, that this assent and ratification is to be given by the people, not as individuals composing one entire nation, but as composing the distinct and independent States to which they respectively belong. It is to be the assent and ratification of the several States, derived from the supreme authority in each State, the authority of the people themselves. The act, therefore, establishing the Constitution, will not be a NATIONAL, but a FEDERAL act.

That it will be a federal and not a national act, as these terms are understood by the objectors; the act of the people, as forming so many independent States, not as forming one aggregate nation, is obvious from this single consideration, that it is to result neither from the decision of a MAJORITY of the people of the Union, nor from that of a MAJORITY of the States. It must result from the UNANIMOUS assent of the several States that are parties to it, differing no otherwise from their ordinary assent than in its being expressed, not by the legislative authority, but by that of the people themselves. Were the people regarded in this transaction as forming one nation, the will of the majority of the whole people of the United States would bind the minority, in the same manner as the majority in each State must bind the minority; and the will of the majority must be determined either by a comparison of the individual votes, or by considering the will of the majority of the States as evidence of the will of a majority of the people of the United States. Neither of these rules have been adopted. Each State, in ratifying the Constitution, is considered as a sovereign body, independent of all others, and only to be bound by its own voluntary act. In this relation, then, the new Constitution will, if established, be a FEDERAL, and not a NATIONAL constitution.

The next relation is, to the sources from which the ordinary powers of government are to be derived. The House of Representatives will derive its powers from the people of America; and the people will be represented in the same proportion, and on the same principle, as they are in the legislature of a particular State. So far the government is NATIONAL, not FEDERAL. The Senate, on the other hand, will derive its powers from the States, as political and coequal societies; and these will be represented on the principle of equality in the Senate, as they now are in the existing Congress. So far the government is FEDERAL, not NATIONAL. The executive power will be derived from a very compound source. The immediate election of the President is to be made by the States in their political characters. The votes allotted to them are in a compound ratio, which considers them partly as distinct and coequal societies, partly as unequal members of the same society. The eventual election, again, is to be made by that branch of the legislature which consists of the national representatives; but in this particular act they are to be thrown into the form of individual delegations, from so many distinct and coequal bodies politic. From this aspect of the government it appears to be of a mixed character, presenting at least as many FEDERAL as NATIONAL features.

The difference between a federal and national government, as it relates to the OPERATION OF THE GOVERNMENT, is supposed to consist in this, that in the former the powers operate on the political bodies composing the Confederacy, in their political capacities; in the latter, on the individual citizens composing the nation, in their individual capacities. On trying the Constitution by this criterion, it falls under the NATIONAL, not the FEDERAL character; though perhaps not so completely as has been understood. In several cases, and particularly in the trial of controversies to which States may be parties, they must be viewed and proceeded against in their collective and political capacities only. So far the national countenance of the government on this side seems to be disfigured by a few federal features. But this blemish is perhaps unavoidable in any plan; and the operation of the government on the people, in their individual capacities, in its ordinary and most essential proceedings, may, on the whole, designate it, in this relation, a NATIONAL government.

But if the government be national with regard to the OPERATION of its powers, it changes its aspect again when we contemplate it in relation to the EXTENT of its powers. The idea of a national government involves in it, not only an authority over the individual citizens, but an indefinite supremacy over all persons and things, so far as they are objects of lawful government. Among a people consolidated into one nation, this supremacy is completely vested in the national legislature. Among communities united for particular purposes, it is vested partly in the general and partly in the municipal legislatures. In the former case, all local authorities are subordinate to the supreme; and may be controlled, directed, or abolished by it at pleasure. In the latter, the local or municipal authorities form distinct and independent portions of the supremacy, no more subject, within their respective spheres, to the general authority, than the general authority is subject to them, within its own sphere. In this relation, then, the proposed government cannot be deemed a NATIONAL one; since its jurisdiction extends to certain enumerated objects only, and leaves to the several States a residuary and inviolable sovereignty over all other objects. It is true that in controversies relating to the boundary between the two jurisdictions, the tribunal which is ultimately to decide, is to be established under the general government. But this does not change the principle of the case. The decision is to be impartially made, according to the rules of the Constitution; and all the usual and most effectual precautions are taken to secure this impartiality. Some such tribunal is clearly essential to prevent an appeal to the sword and a dissolution of the compact; and that it ought to be established under the general rather than under the local governments, or, to speak more properly, that it could be safely established under the first alone, is a position not likely to be combated.

If we try the Constitution by its last relation to the authority by which amendments are to be made, we find it neither wholly NATIONAL nor wholly FEDERAL. Were it wholly national, the supreme and ultimate authority would reside in the MAJORITY of the people of the Union; and this authority would be competent at all times, like that of a majority of every national society, to alter or abolish its established government. Were it wholly federal, on the other hand, the concurrence of each State in the Union would be essential to every alteration that would be binding on all. The mode provided by the plan of the convention is not founded on either of these principles. In requiring more than a majority, and principles. In requiring more than a majority, and particularly in computing the proportion by STATES, not by CITIZENS, it departs from the NATIONAL and advances towards the FEDERAL character; in rendering the concurrence of less than the whole number of States sufficient, it loses again the FEDERAL and partakes of the NATIONAL character.

The proposed Constitution, therefore, is, in strictness, neither a national nor a federal Constitution, but a composition of both. In its foundation it is federal, not national; in the sources from which the ordinary powers of the government are drawn, it is partly federal and partly national; in the operation of these powers, it is national, not federal; in the extent of them, again, it is federal, not national; and, finally, in the authoritative mode of introducing amendments, it is neither wholly federal nor wholly national.

PUBLIUS.

Appendix B - Comparison of the U.S. and C.S.A. Constitutions

THE CONSTITUTION OF THE CONFEDERATE STATES OF AMERICA

By J.J. McCullough

What was changed? And why?

In February of 1861 six states seceded from the United States of America and declared themselves independent. They formed a new, rival country known as the **Confederate States of America**. In the months that followed, seven more American states followed suit, slicing the former United States into two clearly-divided rival factions.

The Civil War that followed, in which the armies of the Confederacy fought the armies of the remaining United States, is one of the seminal events of American history. But why was the Civil War even fought in the first place? Heck, why did the Confederacy even exist?

Modern-day Confederate apologists insist the Southern states only separated in response to legitimate political grievances, namely that the South's capacity for self-government was being unjustly restrained by a tyrannical federal government dominated by northern politicians who had no respect for "states' rights," federalism, and local sovereignty. Everyone else insists the Confederacy was founded for a much less noble reason, namely to keep slavery legal at a time when the rest of country was uniting against the practice.

We can get a good glimpse into the founding principles of the Confederacy by taking an in-depth look at the Confederate constitution, which was approved, and came into use by the rebel states on March 11, 1861. The document is largely a word-for-word copy of the United States constitution, but with several key changes. The changes offer the clearest window of insight into how precisely the CSA intended to be different from the USA, and why.

THE CHANGES

Before we get into a line-by-line comparison, I should point out the minor, mostly cosmetic changes that occurred during the revision process:

- All references to the "United States" were changed to the "Confederate States;" references to the "Union" were changed to "Confederacy."
- The CSA's constitution's punctuation, capitalization, and in some cases spelling, are all updated from 18th Century to 19th Century English standards.
- The CSA constitution numbers its clauses. In most cases, each paragraph from the US constitution is numbered as a single clause, but in some cases the CSA merges multiple clauses into one big one, or breaks up long paragraphs into several smaller ones.

On the comparison chart below, note that in the CSA column indicates new additions to original US clauses. NOTE: The original for this information can be found on the website below. The only changes made were to get the data into the correct format for the publisher.

http://www.jjmccullough.com/CSA.htm

USA	CSA	Notes
We the People of the United States, in Order to form a more perfect Union, establish Justice, insure domestic Tranquility, provide for the common defense, promote the general Welfare, and secure the Blessings of Liberty to ourselves and our Posterity, do ordain and establish this Constitution for the United States of America.	We, the people of the Confederate States, each State acting in its sovereign and independent character, in order to form a permanent federal government, establish justice, insure domestic tranquility, and secure the blessings of liberty to ourselves and our posterity — invoking the favor and guidance of Almighty God — do ordain and establish this Constitution for the Confederate States of America.	The Confederacy's preamble more-or-less deleted any reference to collective interests, presumably because it ostensibly intended to be a country focused more on state independence than any sort of grander, national goal. The CSA does not promise to form a "perfect union" nor does it aspire to provide for the "common defense" or promote the "general welfare." It does, however, explicitly evoke God. So there would be no ACLU court challenges about the Pledge of Allegiance in alternate CSA-won-the-Civil-War-world.
	Article I	
Section. 1. [Legislative Branch]	**Section. 1. [Legislative Branch]**	
All legislative Powers herein granted shall be vested in a Congress of the United States, which shall consist	All legislative powers herein delegated shall be vested in a Congress of the Confederate States, which shall consist of a Senate and House of	Changed the world "granted" to "delegated," which I suppose makes the federal government seem slightly more gentle and conciliatory.

USA	CSA	Notes
of a Senate and House of Representatives.	Representatives.	
Section. 2. [House]	**Section. 2. [House]**	
The House of Representatives shall be composed of Members chosen every second Year by the People of the several States, and the Electors in each State shall have the Qualifications requisite for Electors of the most numerous Branch of the State Legislature.	(1) The House of Representatives shall be composed of members chosen every second year by the people of the several States; and the electors in each State shall be citizens of the Confederate States, and have the qualifications requisite for electors of the most numerous branch of the State Legislature; but no person of foreign birth, not a citizen of the Confederate States, shall be allowed to vote for any officer, civil or political, State or Federal.	The Confederacy explicitly declares that only citizens of the CSA can vote in elections. In the USA the individual states have the power to decide voter eligibility
No Person shall be a Representative who shall not have attained to the Age of twenty five Years, and been seven Years a Citizen of the United States, and who shall not, when elected, be an Inhabitant of that	(2) No person shall be a Representative who shall not have attained the age of twenty-five years, and be a citizen of the Confederate States, and who shall not when elected, be an inhabitant of that State in which he shall be chosen.	Since the CSA was just being created, the Confederacy could not demand that their Representatives be citizens for seven years. The USA could, because at the time their constitution was adopted the US had already existed for almost ten years under

USA	CSA	Notes
State in which he shall be chosen.		the Articles of Confederation.
Representatives and direct Taxes shall be apportioned among the several States which may be included within this Union, according to their respective Numbers, which shall be determined by adding to the whole Number of free Persons, including those bound to Service for a Term of Years, and excluding Indians not taxed, three fifths of all other Persons. The actual Enumeration shall be made within three Years after Years after the first Meeting of the Congress of the United States, and within every subsequent Term of ten Years, in such Manner as they shall by Law direct. The Number of Representatives shall not exceed one for every thirty	(3) Representatives and direct taxes shall be apportioned among the several States, which may be included within this Confederacy, according to their respective numbers, which shall be determined by adding to the whole number of free persons, including those bound to service for a term of years, and excluding Indians not taxed, three-fifths of all slaves. The actual enumeration shall be made within three years after the first meeting of the Congress of the Confederate States, and within every subsequent term of ten years, in such manner as they shall by law direct. The number of Representatives shall not exceed one for every fifty thousand, but each State shall have at least one Representative; and until such enumeration shall be made, the State of South	This is a complicated clause detailing how to measure the population of the states. At the time, the US formally regarded slaves as only counting as "three fifths" of a person, which allowed the non-slave states to be over-represented in the Congress. The CSA kept this rule for some reason, probably to even out representatives among their slave-heavy and slave-light states. The US constitution also bent over backwards to avoid using the term "slave" or "slavery" in the document, but the pro-slavery CSA apparently didn't have a problem calling a spade a spade. Lastly, the CSA appeared to aspire to have a smaller Congress, as Representatives could represent up to 50,000 people, while in the US the max is 30,000 per

USA	CSA	Notes
Thousand, but each State shall have at Least one Representative; and until such enumeration shall be made, the State of New Hampshire shall be entitled to choose three, Massachusetts eight, Rhode-Island and Providence Plantations one, Connecticut five, New York six, New Jersey four, Pennsylvania eight, Delaware one, Maryland six, Virginia ten, North Carolina five, South Carolina five, and Georgia three.	Carolina shall be entitled to choose six; the State of Georgia ten; the State of Alabama nine; the State of Florida two; the State of Mississippi seven; the State of Louisiana six; and the State of Texas six.	Congressman. And obviously the founding states are different.
When vacancies happen in the Representation from any State, the executive authority thereof shall issue Writs of Election to fill such Vacancies.	(4) When vacancies happen in the repre-sentation from any State the executive authority thereof shall issue writs of election to fill such vacancies.	No changes.
The House of Representatives shall choose their Speaker and other Officers; and shall have the sole Power of Impeachment.	(5) The House of Representatives shall choose their Speaker and other officers; and shall have the sole power of	The CSA gave state legislatures the power to impeach federally-appointed state court judges and other federally- appointed state Officials.

79

USA	CSA	Notes
	impeachment; except that any judicial or other Federal officer, resident and acting solely within the limits of any State, may be impeached by a vote of two-thirds of both branches of the Legislature thereof.	This is relevant as some federal judicial districts at the time (and today) exist only within a single state, yet state governments are powerless to control them, because they are federal employees. This change thus gives (certain) states more power over their presiding federal judges, which in turn blurs the distinction between federal and state judicial authority.
Section. 3. (Senate)	**Section. 3. (Senate)**	
The Senate of the United States shall be composed of two Senators from each State, chosen by the Legislature thereof for six Years; and each Senator shall have one Vote.	(1) The Senate of the Confederate States shall be composed of two Senators from each State, chosen for six years by the Legislature thereof, at the regular session next immediately preceding the commencement of the term of service; and each Senator shall have one vote.	The CSA clarifies that state legislatures will appoint senators at the last session before the Senator's term expires. This prevented state legislatures from appointing a "reserve" senator to wait in the wings until the incumbent guy left office, as was common in some American states.
Immediately after they shall be assembled in Consequence of the first Election, they shall be divided as equally as may be into three Classes.	(2) Immediately after they shall be assembled, in consequence of the first election, they shall be divided as equally as may be into three classes.	No changes.

USA	CSA	Notes
The Seats of the Senators of the first Class shall be vacated at the Expiration of the second Year, of the second Class at the Expiration of the fourth Year, and of the third Class at the Expiration of the sixth Year, so that one third may be chosen every second Year; and if Vacancies happen by Resignation, or otherwise, during the recess of the Legislature of any State, the Executive thereof may make temporary Appointments until the next meeting of the Legislature, which shall then fill such Vacancies.	The seats of the Senators of the first class shall be vacated at the expiration of the second year; of the second class at the expiration of the fourth year; and of the third class at the expiration of the sixth year; so that one-third may be chosen every second year; and if vacancies happen by resignation, or otherwise, during the recess of the Legislature of any State, the Executive thereof may make temporary appointments until the next meeting of the Legislature, which shall then fill such vacancies.	
No Person shall be a Senator who shall not have attained to the Age of thirty Years, and been nine Years a Citizen of the United States,	(3) No person shall be a Senator who shall not have attained the age of thirty years, and be a citizen of the Confederate States; and who shall not,	Again, the CSA is too young to demand nine years of citizenship from its senators.

USA	CSA	Notes
and who shall not, when elected, be an Inhabitant of that State for which he shall be chosen.	then elected, be an inhabitant of the State for which he shall be chosen.	
The Vice President of the United States shall be President of the Senate, but shall have no Vote, unless they be equally divided.	(4) The Vice President of the Confederate States shall be president of the Senate, but shall have no vote unless they be equally divided.	No changes.
The Senate shall choose their other Officers, and also a President pro tempore, in the Absence of the Vice President, or when he shall exercise the Office of President of the United States.	(5) The Senate shall choose their other officers; and also a president pro tempore in the absence of the Vice President, or when he shall exercise the office of President of the Confederate states.	No changes.
The Senate shall have the sole Power to try all Impeachments. When sitting for that Purpose, they shall be on Oath or Affirmation. When the President of the United States is tried, the Chief Justice shall preside: And no Person shall be	(6) The Senate shall have the sole power to try all impeachments. When sitting for that purpose, they shall be on oath or affirmation. When the President of the Confederate States is tried, the Chief Justice shall preside; and no person shall be	No changes.

USA	CSA	Notes
convicted without the Concurrence of two thirds of the Members present.	convicted without the concurrence of two-thirds of the members present.	
Judgment in Cases of Impeachment shall not extend further than to removal from Office, and disqualification to hold and enjoy any Office of honor, Trust or Profit under the United States: but the Party convicted shall nevertheless be liable and subject to Indictment, Trial, Judgment and Punishment, according to Law.	(7) Judgment in cases of impeachment shall not extend further than to removal from office, and disqualification to hold any office of honor, trust, or profit under the Confederate States; but the party convicted shall, nevertheless, be liable and subject to indictment, trial, judgment, and punishment according to law.	No changes.
Section. 4.	**Section. 4.**	
The Times, Places & Manner of holding Elections for Senators and Representatives, shall be prescribed in each State by the Legislature thereof; but the Congress may at any time by Law make or alter such Regulations, except as to the Places of choosing Senators.	(1) The times, places, & manner of holding elections for Senators and Representatives shall be prescribed in each State by the Legislature thereof, subject to the provisions of this Constitution; but the Congress may, at any time, by law, make or alter such regulations, except as to the times and	The CSA adds a disclaimer that the state legislatures are bound by the federal constitution when creating rules for elections to the Senate and House. This evokes Section 2(1) of the Confederate constitution, which demands that states only grant voting rights to citizens. The CSA also takes away the Congress' power to alter the time of choosing Senators, as the

USA	CSA	Notes
	places of choosing Senators.	CSA constitution already sets out a specific timeframe for appointments in Section 3(1).
The Congress shall assemble at least once in every Year, and such Meeting shall be on the first Monday in December, unless they shall by Law appoint a different Day.	(2) The Congress shall assemble at least once in every year; and such meeting shall be on the first Monday in December, unless they shall, by law, appoint a different day.	No changes.
Section. 5.	**Section. 5.**	
Each House shall be the Judge of the Elections, Returns and Qualifications of its own Members, and a Majority of each shall constitute a Quorum to do Business; but a smaller Number may adjourn from day to day, and may be authorized to compel the Attendance of absent Members, in such Manner, and under such Penalties as each House may provide.	(1) Each House shall be the judge of the elections, returns, and qualifications of its own members, and a majority of each shall constitute a quorum to do business; but a smaller number may adjourn from day to day, and may be authorized to compel the attendance of absent members in such manner and under such penalties as each House may provide.	No changes.

USA	CSA	Notes
Each House may determine the Rules of its Proceedings, punish its Members for disorderly Behaviour, and, with the Concurrence of two thirds, expel a Member.	(2) Each House may determine the rules of its proceedings, punish its members for disorderly behavior, and, with the concurrence of two-thirds of the whole number, expel a member.	No changes.
Each House shall keep a Journal of its Proceedings, and from time to time publish the same, excepting such Parts as may in their judgment require Secrecy; and the Yeas and Nays of the Members of either House on any question shall, at the Desire of one fifth of those Present, be entered on the Journal.	(3) Each House shall keep a journal of its proceedings, and from time to time publish the same, excepting such parts as may in their judgment require secrecy; and the yeas and nays of the members of either House, on any question, shall, at the desire of one-fifth of those present, be entered on the journal.	No changes.
Section. 6.	**Section. 6.**	
The Senators and Representatives shall receive a Compensation for their Services, to be ascertained by Law, and paid out of the Treasury of the United States. They shall in all	(1) The Senators and Representatives shall receive a compensation for their services, to be ascertained by law, and paid out of the Treasury of the Confederate States. They shall, in all	Two of the US constitution's original clauses are merged into one big clause here. Most of the content is unchanged.... but the CSA tacks on a bit at the end, which introduces a

USA	CSA	Notes
cases, except Treason, Felony and Breach of the Peace, be privileged from Arrest during their Attendance at the Session of their respective Houses, and in going to and returning from the same; and for any Speech or Debate in either House, they shall not be questioned in any other Place. No Senator or Representative shall, during the Time for which he was elected, be appointed to any civil Office under the Authority of the United States, which shall have been created, or the Emoluments whereof shall have been increased during such time; and no Person holding any Office under the United States, shall be a Member of either House during his Continuance in Office.	cases, except treason, felony, and breach of the peace, be privileged from arrest during their attendance at the session of their respective Houses, and in going to and returning from the same; and for any speech or debate in either House, they shall not be question-ed in any other place. No Senator or Repre-sentative shall, during the time for which he was elected, be ap-pointed to any civil office under the authority of the Confederate States, which shall have been created, or the emoluments whereof shall have been increased during such time; and no person holding any office under the Confederate States shall be a member of either House during his continuance in office. But Congress may, by law, grant to the principal	pseudo-parliamentary reform to the Congress. Under the CSA system, cabinet secretaries can be given a "seat" in either house of Congress in order to answer direct questions from members. This is actually not that different than what happens today, when Cabinet Secretaries can be summoned to answer questions before a Congressional committee.

USA	CSA	Notes
	officer in each of the Executive Departments a seat upon the floor of either House, with the privilege of discussing any measures appertaining to his department.	
Section. 7.	**Section. 7.**	
All Bills for raising Revenue shall originate in the House of Representatives; but the Senate may propose or concur with Amendments as on other Bills.	(1) All bills for raising revenue shall originate in the House of Representatives; but the Senate may propose or concur with amendments, as on other bills.	No changes.
Every Bill which shall have passed the House of Representatives and the Senate, shall, before it become a Law, be presented to the President of the United States: If he approve he shall sign it, but if not he shall return it, with his Objections to that House in which it shall have originated, who shall enter the Objections at large on their Journal, and proceed to	(2) Every bill which shall have passed both Houses, shall, before it becomes a law, be presented to the President of the Confederate States; if he approve, he shall sign it; but if not, he shall return it, with his objections, to that House in which it shall have originated, who shall enter the objections at large on their journal, and proceed to reconsider it. If, after such re-	This is the longest clause in the constitution and the Confederates added quite a bit to the end. The bulk of the clause explains how the Congress can override the president's veto. The Confederates alter this a bit, and give the CSA president the power to approve *certain* parts of a bill into law, and reject other parts. Today this power is known as a "line-item veto." Many US state governors have such a power, but the American president does not.

USA	CSA	Notes
reconsider it. If after such Reconsideration two thirds of that House shall agree to pass the Bill, it shall be sent, together with the Objections, to the other House, by which it shall likewise be re-considered, and if approved by two thirds of that House, it shall become a Law. But in all such Cases the Votes of both Houses shall be determined by yeas and Nays, and the Names of the Persons voting for and against the Bill shall be entered on the Journal of each House respectively. If any Bill shall not be returned by the President within ten Days (Sundays excepted) after it shall have been presented to him, the Same shall be a Law, in like Manner as if he had signed it, unless the Congress by their	consideration, two-thirds of that House shall agree to pass the bill, it shall be sent, together with the objections, to the other House, by which it shall likewise be re-considered, and if approved by two-thirds of that House, it shall become a law. But in all such cases, the votes of both Houses shall be determined by yeas and nays, and the names of the per-sons voting for and against the bill shall be entered on the journal of each House respectively. If any bill shall not be re-turned by the President within ten days (Sundays excepted) after it shall have been presented to him, the same shall be a law, in like manner as if he had signed it, unless the Congress, by their ad-journment, prevent its return; in which case it shall not be a law. The President	

USA	CSA	Notes
Adjournment prevent its Return, in which Case it shall not be a Law.	may approve any appropriation and disapprove any other appropriation in the same bill. In such case he shall, in signing the bill, designate the appropriations disapproved; and shall return a copy of such appropriations, with his objections, to the House in which the bill shall have originated; and the same proceedings shall then be had as in case of other bills disapproved by the President.	
Every Order, Resolution, or Vote to which the Concurrence of the Senate and House of Representatives may be necessary (except on a question of Adjournment) shall be presented to the President of the United States; and before the Same shall take Effect, shall be approved by him, or being disapproved by	(3) Every order, resolution, or vote, to which the concurrence of both Houses may be necessary (except on a question of adjournment) shall be presented to the President of the Confederate States; and before the same shall take effect, shall be approved by him; or, being disapproved by him, shall be repassed by two-thirds of both	One of the few minor meaningless wording changes.

USA	CSA	Notes
him, shall be repassed by two thirds of the Senate and House of Representatives, according to the Rules and Limitations prescribed in the Case of a Bill.	Houses, according to the rules and limitations prescribed in case of a bill.	
Section. 8.	**Section. 8. The Congress shall have power.**	
The Congress shall have Power To lay and collect Taxes, Duties, Imposts and Excises, to pay the Debts and provide for the common Defense and general Welfare of the United States; but all Duties, Imposts and Excises shall be uniform throughout the United States;	(1) To lay and collect taxes, duties, imposts, and excises for revenue, necessary to pay the debts, provide for the common defense, and carry on the Government of the Confederate States; but no bounties shall be granted from the Treasury; nor shall any duties or taxes on importations from foreign nations be laid to promote or foster any branch of industry; and all duties, imposts, and excises shall be uniform throughout the Confederate States.	In the CSA constitution Section 8 has an official title: "Congress shall have power", where as in the original it's much less organized.

The Confederates didn't mention "providing for the common defense" in their constitution's pre-amble, but they do here. "General welfare" is still omitted, preamble, but they do here. "General welfare" is still omitted, however. Instead we get "carry on the Government." Lastly, the CSA essentially bans trade protectionism by saying that tariffs cannot be imposed on foreign goods for the sole purpose of protecting local industry. |

USA	CSA	Notes
		It also bans "bounties" from the Treasury, which at the time was the term used to describe government subsidies distributed to offset the costs of managing certain uncompetitive industries. Southerners had often been prevented from buying cheaper foreign goods because of such Yankee protectionist measures.
To borrow Money on the credit of the United States;	(2) To borrow money on the credit of the Confederate States.	No changes.
To regulate Commerce with foreign Nations, and among the several States, and with the Indian Tribes;	(3) To regulate commerce with foreign nations, and among the several States, and with the Indian tribes; but neither this, nor any other clause contained in the Constitution, shall ever be construed to delegate the power to Congress to appropriate money for any internal improvement intended to facilitate commerce; except for the purpose of	The Confederates added a ton here. The changes basically place limits on the sort of infrastructure spending Congress can authorize, which the Confederates don't seem very big on. More important is the latter comment about "duties" to be laid upon those who use Confederate waterways — this was seen as an important way for the new country to raise revenue.

USA	CSA	Notes
	furnishing lights, beacons, and buoys, and other aids to navigation upon the coasts, and the improvement of harbors and the removing of obstructions in river navigation; in all which cases such duties shall be laid on the navigation facilitated thereby as may be ne-cessary to pay the costs and expenses thereof.	
To establish an uniform Rule of Naturalization, and uniform Laws on the subject of Bankruptcies throughout the United States;	(4) To establish uniform laws of naturalization, and uniform laws on the subject of bankruptcies, throughout the Confederate States; but no law of Congress shall discharge any debt contracted before the passage of the same.	The CSA Congress cannot authorize forgiveness of debts.
To coin Money, regulate the Value thereof, and of foreign Coin, and fix the Standard of Weights and Measures;	(5) To coin money, regulate the value thereof, and of foreign coin, and fix the standard of weights and measures.	No changes.

USA	CSA	Notes
To provide for the punishment of counterfeiting the Securities and current Coin of the USA.	(6) To provide for the punishment of counterfeiting the securities and current coin of the CSA.	No changes.
To establish Post Offices and post Roads;	(7) To establish post offices and post routes; but the expenses of the Post Office Department, after the 1st day of March in the year of our Lord eighteen hundred and sixty-three, shall be paid out of its own revenues.	The Confederates set a cut-off day after which they would no longer provide cash for the Post Office Department. It's also worth noting that the Confederates use the term "year of our Lord" when referencing dates. The US constitution just says "the year."
To promote the Progress of Science and useful Arts, by securing for limited Times to Authors and Inventors the exclusive Right to their respective Writings and Discoveries;	(8) To promote the progress of science and useful arts, by securing for limited times to authors and inventors the exclusive right to their respective writings and discoveries.	No changes.
To constitute Tribunals inferior to the supreme Court;	(9) To constitute tribunals inferior to the Supreme Court.	No changes.
To define and punish Piracies and Felonies committed on the high Seas, and Offences against the Law of Nations;	(10) To define and punish piracies and felonies committed on the high seas, and offenses against the law of nations.	No changes.

USA	CSA	Notes
To declare War, grant Letters of Marque and Reprisal, and make Rules concerning Captures on Land and Water;	(11) To declare war, grant letters of Marque and reprisal, and make rules concerning captures on land and water.	No changes.
To raise and support Armies, but no Appropriation of money to that Use shall be for a longer term than two Years;	(12) To raise and support armies; but no appropriation of money to that use shall be for a longer term than two years.	No changes.
To provide and maintain a Navy;	(13) To provide and maintain a navy.	No changes.
To make Rules for the Government and Regulation of the land and naval Forces;	(14) To make rules for the government and regulation of the land and naval forces.	No changes.
To provide for calling forth the Militia to execute the Laws of the Union, suppress Insurrections and repel Invasions;	(15) To provide for calling forth the militia to execute the laws of the Confederate States, suppress insurrections, and repel invasions.	No changes. By keeping this clause the CSA essentially gives itself the right to fight its own Civil War someday.
To provide for organizing, arming, and disciplining, the Militia, and for governing such Part of them as may be employed in the Service of the United States, reserving to the States respectively,	(16) To provide for organizing, arming, and disciplining the militia, and for governing such part of them as may be employed in the service of the Confederate States; reserving to the States, respectively,	No changes.

94

USA	CSA	Notes
the Appointment of the Officers, and the Authority of training the Militia according to the discipline prescribed by Congress;	the appointment of the officers, and the authority of training the militia according to the discipline prescribed by Congress.	
To exercise exclusive Legislation in all Cases whatsoever, over such District (not exceeding ten Miles square) as may, by Cession of particular States, and the Acceptance of Congress, become the Seat of the Government of the United States, and to exercise like Authority over all Places purchased by the Consent of the Legislature of the State in which the Same shall be, for the Erection of Forts, Magazines, Arsenals, dock-Yards, and other needful Buildings;--And	(17) To exercise exclusive legislation, in all cases whatsoever, over such district (not exceeding ten miles square) as may, by cession of one or more States and the acceptance of Congress, become the seat of the Government of the Confederate States; and to exercise like authority over all places purchased by the consent of the Legislature of the State in which the same shall be, for the erection of forts, magazines, arsenals, dockyards, and other needful buildings; and	The Confederacy makes the meaningless clarification that "one or more" states can give up territory to provide the country's capital district. Trivia question: what was the capital district of the CSA? Answer: they never had time to make one.
To make all Laws which shall be necessary and proper for carrying	(18) To make all laws which shall be necessary and proper for carrying	No changes. It's interesting to note how the Confederacy barely takes away any powers from the

USA	CSA	Notes
into Execution the foregoing Powers, and all other Powers vested by this Constitution in the Government of the United States, or in any Department or Officer thereof.	into execution the foregoing powers, and all other powers vested by this Constitution in the Government of the Confederate States, or in any department or officer thereof.	federal government.
Section. 9.	**Section. 9.**	
The Migration or Importation of such Persons as any of the States now existing shall think proper to admit, shall not be prohibited by the Congress prior to the Year one thousand eight hundred and eight, but a Tax or duty may be imposed on such Importation, not exceeding ten dollars for each Person.	(1) The importation of negroes of the African race from any foreign country other than the slaveholding States or Territories of the United States of America, is hereby forbidden; and Congress is required to pass such laws as shall effectually prevent the same.	This clause is an updated version of what was originally a time-sensitive article in the US constitution. The original US Section 9(1), in its euphemistic language, stated that Congress could only ban the slave trade after 1808 (and they did). The Confederate clause 9(1) makes this ban on the slave trade permanent, though slave trading with the US is still permitted. Curiously, the clause also "requires" Congress to pass anti-slave trading laws to further outlaw some-thing that's unconstitutional anyway.
N/A	(2) Congress shall also have power to prohibit the introduction of slaves from any State not a member of, or Territory not	This clause was a completely new addition, the first of a few. It gives Congress the power to ban slave imports from

USA	CSA	Notes
	belonging to, this Confederacy.	*specific* US states and territories, should they ever desire to do so. This clause is thus a clever loophole of sorts, in that it allows the CSA to ban slave imports from the US while simultaneously not contradicting clause 1.
The Privilege of the Writ of Habeas Corpus shall not be suspended, unless when in Cases of Rebellion or Invasion the public Safety may require it.	(3) The privilege of the writ of habeas corpus shall not be suspended, unless when in cases of rebellion or invasion the public safety may require it.	No changes. Though Confederate apologists often bemoan the fact that the Yankee tyrant Lincoln suspended habeus corpus, there was nothing to stop the President of the Confederacy from doing the exact same thing.
No Bill of Attainder or ex post facto Law shall be passed.	(4) No bill of attainder, ex post facto law, or law denying or im-pairing the right of property in negro slaves shall be passed.	The most important clause in the entire CSA constitution: the right to own slaves.
No Capitation, or other direct, Tax shall be laid, unless in Proportion to the Census or enumeration herein before directed to be taken.	(5) No capitation or other direct tax shall be laid, unless in proportion to the census or enum-eration herein before directed to be taken.	No changes.
No Tax or Duty shall be laid on	(6) No tax or duty shall be laid on	The Confederate Congress gains the power to meddle in

USA	CSA	Notes
Articles exported from any State.	articles exported from any State, except by a vote of two-thirds of both Houses.	the free-trading between the states by imposing tariffs on certain states' exported goods. The Confederates were eyeing another possible source of revenue.
No Preference shall be given by any Regulation of Commerce or Revenue to the Ports of one State over those of an-other; nor shall Vessels bound to, or from, one State, be obliged to enter, clear, or pay Duties in another.	(7) No preference shall be given by any regulation of commerce or revenue to the ports of one State over those of another.	The CSA ditches the last sentence of the American clause, thus giving its states the power to tax domestic ships who enter their ports. The reason? See above.
No Money shall be drawn from the Treasury, but in Consequence of Appropriations made by Law; and a regular Statement and Account of the Receipts and Expenditures of all public Money shall be published from time to time.	(8) No money shall be drawn from the Treasury, but in consequence of appropriations made by law; and a regular statement and account of the receipts and expenditures of all public money shall be published from time to time.	No changes.
N/A	(9) Congress shall appropriate no money from the	The first of two new Confederate clauses that try to impose certain standards of

USA	CSA	Notes
	Treasury except by a vote of two-thirds of both Houses, taken by yeas and nays, unless it be asked and estimated for by some one of the heads of departments and submitted to Congress by the President; or for the purpose of paying its own expenses and contingencies; or for the payment of claims against the Confederate States, the justice of which shall have been judicially declared by a tribunal for the investigation of claims against the Government, which it is hereby made the duty of Congress to establish.	fiscal responsibility on the legislative branch. The CSA Congress can only appropriate cash: • in response to a specific request from the executive branch • to pay for its own expenses • to pay for the national debt and other financial "claims" against the national government The document also demands that the Confederate Congress establish a tribunal to "investigate" the validity of such claims made against the CSA.
N/A	(10) All bills appropriating money shall specify in Federal currency the exact amount of each appropriation and the purposes for which it is made; and	The CSA Congress is forced to only issue money bills that cite an exact dollar amount, and cannot grant a penny more after such a bill is passed.

USA	CSA	Notes
	Congress shall grant no extra compensation to any public contractor, officer, agent, or servant, after such contract shall have been made or such service rendered.	
No Title of Nobility shall be granted by the United States: And no Person holding any Office of Profit or Trust under them, shall, without the Consent of the Congress, accept of any present, Emolument, Office, or Title, of any kind whatever, from any King, Prince, or foreign State.	(11) No title of nobility shall be granted by the Confederate States; and no person holding any office of profit or trust under them shall, without the consent of the Congress, accept of any present, emolument, office, or title of any kind whatever, from any king, prince, or foreign state.	No changes.
[Amendment I, see note at right] Congress shall make no law respecting an establishment of religion, or prohibiting the free exercise thereof; or	(12) Congress shall make no law respecting an establishment of religion, or prohibiting the free exercise thereof; or abridging the freedom of speech, or of the press; or	The CSA constitution directly incorporates the Bill of Rights into their constitution, which only makes sense. The original Bill of Rights takes the form of 10 amendments tacked to the end of the US constitution (cited here, out of place). This part of the CSA constitution only includes the

USA	CSA	Notes
abridging the freedom of speech, or of the press; or the right of the people peaceably to assemble, and to petition the Government for a redress of grievances.	the right of the people peaceably to assemble and petition the Government for a redress of grievances.	first eight Bill of Rights amendments, the last two are included at the very end of the document.
[Amendment II] A well regulated Militia, being necessary to the security of a free State, the right of the people to keep and bear Arms, shall not be infringed.	(13) A well-regulated militia being necessary to the security of a free State, the right of the people to keep and bear arms shall not be infringed.	Though there are no changes per se, Second Amendment scholars in the US have long argued over the significance of the punctuation in this clause. The CSA's version gets rid of a few commas, which makes the language closer to what gun control advocates believe the amendment was *supposed* to say, namely that the right to keep and bear arms only exists if one belongs to a militia.
[Amendment III] No Soldier shall, in time of peace be quartered in any house, without the consent of the Owner, nor in time of war, but in a manner to be prescribed by law.	(14) No soldier shall, in time of peace, be quartered in any house without the consent of the owner; nor in time of war, but in a manner to be prescribed by law.	No changes.

USA	CSA	Notes
[Amendment IV] The right of the people to be secure in their persons, houses, papers, and effects, against unreasonable searches and seizures, shall not be violated, and no Warrants shall issue, but upon probable cause, supported by Oath or affirmation, and particularly describing the place to be searched, and the persons or things to be seized.	(15) The right of the people to be secure in their persons, houses, papers, and effects, against unreasonable searches and seizures, shall not be violated; and no warrants shall issue but upon probable cause, supported by oath or affirmation, and particularly describing the place to be searched and the persons or things to be seized.	No changes.
[Amendment V] No person shall be held to answer for a capital, or otherwise infamous crime, unless on a presentment or indictment of a Grand Jury, except in cases arising in the land or naval forces, or in the	(16) No person shall be held to answer for a capital or otherwise infamous crime, unless on a presentment or indictment of a grand jury, except in cases arising in the land or naval forces, or in the militia, when in actual service in time of war or	No changes.

USA	CSA	Notes
Militia, when in actual service in time of War or public danger; nor shall any person be subject for the same offence to be twice put in jeopardy of life or limb; nor shall be compelled in any criminal case to be a witness against himself, nor be deprived of life, liberty, or property, without due process of law; nor shall private property be taken for public use, without just compensation.	public danger; nor shall any person be subject for the same offense to be twice put in jeopardy of life or limb; nor be compelled, in any criminal case, to be a witness against himself; nor be deprived of life, liberty, or property without due process of law; nor shall private property be taken for public use, without just compensation.	
[Amendment VI] In all criminal prosecutions, the accused shall enjoy the right to a speedy and public trial, by an impartial jury of the State and district wherein the crime shall have been	(17) In all criminal prosecutions the accused shall enjoy the right to a speedy and public trial, by an impartial jury of the State and district wherein the crime shall have been committed, which district shall have been	No changes.

USA	CSA	Notes
committed, which district shall have been previously ascertained by law, and to be informed of the nature and cause of the accusation; to be confronted with the witnesses against him; to have compulsory process for obtaining witnesses in his favor, and to have the Assistance of Counsel for his defense.	previously ascertained by law, and to be informed of the nature and cause of the accusation; to be confronted with the witnesses against him; to have compulsory process for obtaining witnesses in his favor; and to have the assistance of counsel for his defense.	
[Amendment VII] In Suits at common law, where the value in controversy shall exceed twenty dollars, the right of trial by jury shall be preserved, and no fact tried by a jury, shall be otherwise re-examined in any Court of the United States, than according	(18) In suits at common law, where the value in controversy shall exceed twenty dollars, the right of trial by jury shall be preserved; and no fact so tried by a jury shall be otherwise reexamined in any court of the Confederacy, than according to the rules of common law.	No changes.

USA	CSA	Notes
to the rules of the common law.		
[Amendment VIII] Excessive bail shall not be required, nor excessive fines imposed, nor cruel and unusual punishments inflicted.	(19) Excessive bail shall not be required, nor excessive fines imposed, nor cruel and unusual punishments inflicted.	No changes
N/A	(20) Every law, or resolution having the force of law, shall relate to but one subject, and that shall be expressed in the title.	The Confederates add this little clause at the end of Section 9. This is quite an interesting addition, as it demands that all bills only relate to "one subject." This would prevent what we see today, where Congress routinely passes all sorts of extraordinarily complicated "omnibus" bills that regulate dozens of different, unrelated realms at once.
Section. 10.	**Section. 10.**	
No State shall enter into any Treaty, Alliance, or Confederation; grant Letters of Marque and Reprisal; coin Money; emit Bills of Credit; make any Thing but gold and	(1) No State shall enter into any treaty, alliance, or confederation; grant letters of Marque and reprisal; coin money; make anything but gold and silver coin a tender in payment of debts; pass any	The CSA deletes the words "emit bills of credit," thereby allowing its states to issue them. By the standards of the time, this could have given states the right to issue their own paper currency. Today, however, a "bill of credit" is usually just understood to be a government loan of some sort.

USA	CSA	Notes
silver Coin a Tender in Payment of Debts; pass any Bill of Attainder, ex post facto Law, or Law impairing the Obligation of Contracts, or grant any Title of Nobility.	bill of attainder, or ex post facto law, or law impairing the obligation of contracts; or grant any title of nobility.	
No State shall, without the Consent of the Congress, lay any Imposts or Duties on Imports or Exports, except what may be absolutely necessary for executing it's inspection Laws: and the net Produce of all Duties and Imposts, imports, or exports, shall be for the use of the Treasury of the Confederate States; and all such laws shall be subject to the revision and control of Congress.	(2) No State shall, without the consent of the Congress, lay any imposts or duties on imports or exports, except what may be absolutely necessary for executing its inspection laws; and the net produce of all duties and imposts, laid by any State on imports, or exports, shall be for the use of the Treasury of the Confederate States; and all such laws shall be subject to the revision and control of Congress.	No changes.

USA	CSA	Notes
No State shall, without the Consent of Congress, lay any Duty of Tonnage, keep Troops, or Ships of War in time of Peace, enter into any Agreement or Compact with another State, or with a foreign Power, or engage in War, unless actually invaded, or in such imminent Danger as will not admit of delay.	(3) No State shall, without the consent of Congress, lay any duty on tonnage, except on seagoing vessels, for the improvement of its rivers and harbors navigated by the said vessels; but such duties shall not conflict with any treaties of the Confederate States with foreign nations; and any surplus revenue thus derived shall, after making such improvement, be paid into the common treasury. Nor shall any State keep troops or ships of war in time of peace, enter into any agreement or compact with another State, or with a foreign power, or engage in war, unless actually invaded, or in such imminent danger as will not admit of delay. But when any river divides or flows through two or more States they	The CSA threw a lot of qualifications into this one.

The Confederates were quite eager to raise money by taxing ships that used their waterways, so this clause had to be rewritten to allow that.

The Confederate states also gain the power to make river-related treaties with each other. In the US, the federal government regulates bodies of water that overlap multiple states. |

USA	CSA	Notes
	may enter into compacts with each other to improve the navigation thereof.	

	Article II	
Section. 1.	**Section. 1.**	
The executive Power shall be vested in a President of the United States of America. He shall hold his Office during the Term of four Years, and, together with the Vice President, chosen for the same Term, be elected, as follows:	(1) The executive power shall be vested in a President of the Confederate States of America. He and the Vice President shall hold their offices for the term of six years; but the President shall not be re-eligible. The President and Vice President shall be elected as follows:	The Confederate president can only serve a single, six-year term, unlike the US president, who (at the time) could be re-elected forever.

Interestingly, the Confederate vice president *could* be re-elected. |
| Each State shall appoint, in such Manner as the Legislature thereof may direct, a Number of Electors, equal to the whole Number of Senators and Representatives to which the State may be entitled in the Congress: but no Senator or Representative, | (2) Each State shall appoint, in such manner as the Legislature thereof may direct, a number of electors equal to the whole number of Senators and Representatives to which the State may be entitled in the Congress; but no Senator or Representative or person holding an office of trust or profit under the | No changes. |

USA	CSA	Notes
or Person holding an Office of Trust or Profit under the United States, shall be appointed an Elector.	Confederate States shall be appointed an elector.	
[Amendment XII] The Electors shall meet in their respective states and vote by ballot for President and Vice-President, one of whom, at least, shall not be an inhabitant of the same state with themselves; they shall name in their ballots the person voted for as President, and in distinct ballots the person voted for as Vice-President, and they shall make distinct lists of all persons voted for as President, and of all persons voted for as Vice-President, and of the number of	(3) The electors shall meet in their respective States and vote by ballot for President and Vice President, one of whom, at least, shall not be an inhabitant of the same State with themselves; they shall name in their ballots the person voted for as President, and in distinct ballots the person voted for as Vice President, and they shall make distinct lists of all persons voted for as President, and of all persons voted for as Vice President, and of the number of votes for each, which lists they shall sign and certify, and transmit, sealed, to the seat of the Government of. the Confederate States, directed to the	The CSA constitution breaks this clause, originally from the US constitution's 12th amendment, into three parts, but it is otherwise unchanged.

USA	CSA	Notes
votes for each, which lists they shall sign and certify, and transmit sealed to the seat of the government of the United States, directed to the President of the Senate; -- the President of the Senate shall, in the presence of the Senate and House of Representatives, open all the certificates and the votes shall then be counted; -- The person having the greatest number of votes for President, shall be the President, if such number be a majority of the whole number of Electors appointed; and if no person have such majority, then from the persons having the highest numbers not exceeding three	President of the Senate; the President of the Senate shall, in the presence of the Senate and House of Representatives, open all the certificates, and the votes shall then be counted; the person having the greatest number of votes for President shall be the President, if such number be a majority of the whole number of electors appointed; and if no person have such majority, then from the persons having the highest numbers, not exceeding three, on the list of those voted for as President, the House of Representatives shall choose immediately, by ballot, the President. But in choosing the President the votes shall be taken by States ~ the representation from each State having one vote; a quorum for this purpose shall consist of a member or members from	

USA	CSA	Notes
on the list of those voted for as President, the House of Representatives shall choose immediately, by ballot, the President. But in choosing the President, the votes shall be taken by states, the representation from each state having one vote; a quorum for this purpose shall consist of a member or members from two-thirds of the states, and a majority of all the states shall be necessary to a choice. And if the House of Representatives shall not choose a President whenever the right of choice shall devolve upon them, before the fourth day of March next following, then the Vice-	two-thirds of the States, and a majority of all the States shall be necessary to a choice. And if the House of Representatives shall not choose a President, whenever the right of choice shall devolve upon them, before the 4th day of March next following, then the Vice President shall act as President, as in case of the death, or other constitutional disability of the President. (4) The person having the greatest number of votes as Vice President shall be the Vice President, if such number be a majority of the whole number of electors appointed; and if no person have a majority, then, from the two highest numbers on the list, the Senate shall choose the Vice President; a quorum for the purpose shall consist of two-thirds of the whole number of Senators, and a	

USA	CSA	Notes
President shall act as President, as in case of the death or other constitutional disability of the President. The person having the greatest number of votes as Vice-President, shall be the Vice-President, if such number be a majority of the whole number of Electors appointed, and if no person have a majority, then from the two highest numbers on the list, the Senate shall choose the Vice-President; a quorum for the purpose shall consist of two-thirds of the whole number of Senators, and a majority of the whole number shall be necessary to a choice. But no person constitutionally	majority of the whole number shall be necessary to a choice. (5) But no person constitutionally ineligible to the office of President shall be eligible to that of Vice President of the Confederate States.	

USA	CSA	Notes
ineligible to the office of President shall be eligible to that of Vice-President of the United States.		
The Congress may determine the Time of choosing the Electors, and the Day on which they shall give their Votes; which Day shall be the same throughout the United States.	(6) The Congress may determine the time of choosing the electors, and the day on which they shall give their votes; which day shall be the same throughout the Confederate States.	No changes.
No Person except a natural born Citizen, or a Citizen of the United States, at the time of the Adoption of this Constitution, shall be eligible to the Office of President; neither shall any Person be eligible to that Office who shall not have attained to the Age of thirty five Years, and been fourteen Years a	(7) No person except a natural-born citizen of the Confederate; States, or a citizen thereof at the time of the adoption of this Constitution, or a citizen thereof born in the United States prior to the 20th of December, 1860, shall be eligible to the office of President; neither shall any person be eligible to that office who shall not have attained the age of thirty-five years, and been fourteen years a	Once again, the Confederacy has to create various grandfather clauses since no one had been a citizen of the CSA prior to their constitution's ratification. Both the CSA and USA constitutions want only "natural-born citizens" to become president, but both constitutions create a window in which it is possible for immigrants to become president so long as they were citizens at the time the constitution was adopted. The Confederate secretary of state Judah

USA	CSA	Notes
Resident within the United States.	resident within the limits of the Confederate States, as they may exist at the time of his election.	Benjamin, who was born in the British Virgin Islands in 1811, could have been president under these terms.
In Case of the Removal of the President from Office, or of his Death, Resignation, or Inability to discharge the Powers and Duties of the said Office, the Same shall devolve on the Vice President, and the Congress may by Law provide for the Case of Removal, Death, Resignation or Inability, both of the President and Vice President, declaring what Officer shall then act as President, and such Officer shall act accordingly, until the Disability be removed, or a	(8) In case of the removal of the President from office, or of his death, resignation, or inability to discharge the powers and duties of said office, the same shall devolve on the Vice President; and the Congress may, by law, provide for the case of removal, death, resignation, or inability, both of the President and Vice President, declaring what officer shall then act as President; and such officer shall act accordingly until the disability be removed or a President shall be elected.	No changes.

USA	CSA	Notes
President shall be elected.		
The President shall, at stated Times, receive for his Services, a Compensation, which shall neither be increased nor diminished during the Period for which he shall have been elected, and he shall not receive within that Period any other emolument from the United States, or any of them.	(9) The President shall, at stated times, receive for his services a compensation, which shall neither be increased nor diminished during the period for which he shall have been elected; and he shall not receive within that period any other emolument from the Confederate States, or any of them.	No changes.
Before he enter on the Execution of his Office, he shall take the following Oath or Affirmation:-- "I do solemnly swear (or affirm) that I will faithfully execute the Office of President of the United States, and will to the best of my Ability, preserve, protect	(10) Before he enters on the execution of his office he shall take the following oath or affirmation: "I do solemnly swear (or affirm) that I will faithfully execute the office of President of the Confederate States, and will, to the best of my ability, preserve, protect, and defend the Constitution thereof."	No changes.

USA	CSA	Notes
and defend the Constitution of the United States."		
Section. 2.	**Section. 2.**	
The President shall be Commander in Chief of the Army and Navy of the United States, and of the Militia of the several States, when called into the actual Service of the United States; he may require the Opinion, in writing, of the principal Officer in each of the executive Departments, upon any Subject relating to the Duties of their respective Offices, and he shall have Power to grant Reprieves and Pardons for Offences against the United States, except in Cases of Impeachment.	(1) The President shall be Commander-in-Chief of the Army and Navy of the Confederate States, and of the militia of the several States, when called into the actual service of the Confederate States; he may require the opinion, in writing, of the principal officer in each of the Executive Departments, upon any subject relating to the duties of their respective offices; and he shall have power to grant reprieves and pardons for offenses against the Confederate States, except in cases of impeachment.	No Changes.

USA	CSA	Notes
He shall have Power, by and with the Advice and Consent of the Senate, to make Treaties, provided two thirds of the Senators present concur; and he shall nominate, and by and with the Advice and Consent of the Senate, shall appoint Ambassadors, other public Ministers and Consuls, Judges of the supreme Court, and all other Officers of the United States, whose Appointments are not herein otherwise provided for, and which shall be established by Law: but the Congress may by Law vest the Appointment of such inferior Officers, as they think proper, in the President alone, in the	(2) He shall have power, by and with the advice and consent of the Senate, to make treaties; provided two-thirds of the Senators present concur; and he shall nominate, and by and with the advice and consent of the Senate shall appoint, ambassadors, other public ministers and consuls, judges of the Supreme Court, and all other officers of the Confederate States whose appointments are not herein otherwise provided for, and which shall be established by law; but the Congress may, by law, vest the appointment of such inferior officers, as they think proper, in the President alone, in the courts of law, or in the heads of departments.	No changes.

USA	CSA	Notes
Courts of Law, or in the Heads of Departments.		
N/A	(3) The principal officer in each of the Executive Departments, and all persons connected with the diplomatic service, may be removed from office at the pleasure of the President. All other civil officers of the Executive Departments may be removed at any time by the President, or other appointing power, when their services are unnecessary, or for dishonesty, incapacity. Inefficiency, misconduct, or neglect of duty; and when so removed, the removal shall be reported to the Senate, together with the reasons therefore.	The Confederate President is given the power to fire pretty much any civil servant he wishes, from cabinet secretaries on down. He must then inform the Senate of the reasons for the firing. The American president has these powers as well, but they are codified in the various laws establishing the cabinet departments and not in the constitution itself.
The President shall have Power to fill up all Vacancies that may happen during the Recess of the Senate, by	(4) The President shall have power to fill all vacancies that may happen during the recess of the Senate, by granting commissions which shall expire at the end	The CSA adds an additional check to prevent the President from exploiting recess appointments. If someone is rejected by the Senate, the President cannot weasel around it by just making that person a recess

USA	CSA	Notes
granting Commissions which shall expire at the End of their next Session.	of their next session; but no person rejected by the Senate shall be reappointed to the same office during their ensuing recess.	appointment. Bad news, Claire Underwood.
Section. 3.	**Section. 3.**	
He shall from time to time give to the Congress Information of the State of the Union, and recommend to their Consideration such Measures as he shall judge necessary and expedient; he may, on extraordinary Occasions, convene both Houses, or either of them, and in Case of Disagreement between them, with Respect to the Time of Adjournment, he may adjourn them to such Time as he shall think proper; he shall receive Ambassadors and other public	(1) The President shall, from time to time, give to the Congress information of the state of the Confederacy, and recommend to their consideration such measures as he shall judge necessary and expedient; he may, on extra-ordinary occasions, convene both Houses, or either of them; and in case of disagreement between them, with respect to the time of adjournment, he may adjourn them to such time as he shall think proper; he shall receive ambassadors and other public ministers; he shall take care that the laws be faithfully executed, and shall commission all the officers of the Confederate States.	The Confederates were kind enough to clarify as to who this mysterious "he" is.

USA	CSA	Notes
Ministers; he shall take Care that the Laws be faithfully executed, and shall Commission all the Officers of the United States.		
Section. 4.	**Section. 4.**	
The President, Vice President and all civil Officers of the United States, shall be removed from Office on Impeachment for, and Conviction of, Treason, Bribery, or other high Crimes and Misdemeanors.	The President, Vice President, and all civil officers of the Confederate States, shall be removed from office on impeachment for and conviction of treason, bribery, or other high crimes and misdemeanors.	No changes.
Article III		
Section. 1.	**Section. 1.**	
The judicial Power of the United States shall be vested in one supreme Court, and in such inferior Courts as the Congress may from time to time ordain and establish. The Judges, both of	Section 1. (1) The judicial power of the Confederate States shall be vested in one Supreme Court, and in such inferior courts as the Congress may, from time to time, ordain and establish. The judges, both of the Supreme and inferior courts, shall hold their offices	No changes.

USA	CSA	Notes
the supreme and inferior Courts, shall hold their Offices during good Behaviour, and shall, at stated Times, receive for their Services a Compensation, which shall not be diminished during their Continuance in Office.	during good behavior, and shall, at stated times, receive for their services a compensation which shall not be diminished during their continuance in office.	
Section. 2.	**Section. 2.**	
The judicial Power shall extend to all Cases, in Law and Equity, arising under this Constitution, the Laws of the United States, and Treaties made, or which shall be made, under their Authority;--to all Cases affecting Ambassadors, other public Ministers and Consuls;--to all Cases of admiralty and maritime Jurisdiction;--to	(1) The judicial power shall extend to all cases arising under this Constitution, the laws of the Confederate States, and treaties made, or which shall be made, under their authority; to all cases affecting ambassadors, other public ministers and consuls; to all cases of admiralty and maritime jurisdiction; to controversies to which the Confed-erate States shall be a party; to controversies between two or more States; between a State and citizens of	The modifications to this section are based on the 11th Amendment to the US constitution, which enhanced the so-called "sovereign immunity" protection of states from federal lawsuits launched by non-residents. CSA deletes the phrase "in law and equity" from the opening line. The CSA clarifies that a federal court can only hear a lawsuit with between a state and non-residents when the state is the plaintiff, a restriction on federal jurisdiction that is similar to the terms of 11th Amendment but doesn't actually go quite as far.

USA	CSA	Notes
Controversies to which the United States shall be a Party;--to Controversies between two or more States;--between a State and Citizens of another State;--between Citizens of different States;--between Citizens of the same State claiming Lands under Grants of different States, and between a State, or the Citizens thereof, and foreign States, Citizens or Subjects. Amendment XI] The Judicial power of the United States shall not be construed to extend to any suit in law or equity, commenced or prosecuted against one of the United States by Citizens of another State, or	another State, where the State is plaintiff; between citizens claiming lands under grants of different States; and between a State or the citizens thereof, and foreign states, citizens, or subjects; but no State shall be sued by a citizen of a foreign state.	They also reword the Content in which citizens who are claiming multi-state land can sue. Originally the clause specifically says that this power is only available to "citizens of the same state" but the Confederates remove this qualifier so that *any* citizen can sue. Lastly, the CSA notes in this section that that foreigners cannot sue the states in federal court, which is also in the 11th Amendment.

USA	CSA	Notes
by Citizens or Subjects of any Foreign State		
In all Cases affecting Ambassadors, other public Ministers and Consuls, and those in which a State shall be Party, the supreme Court shall have original Jurisdiction. In all the other Cases before mentioned, the supreme Court shall have appellate Jurisdiction, both as to Law and Fact, with such Exceptions, and under such Regulations as the Congress shall make.	(2) In all cases affecting ambassadors, other public ministers and consuls, and those in which a State shall be a party, the Supreme Court shall have original jurisdiction. In all the other cases before mentioned, the Supreme Court shall have appellate jurisdiction both as to law and fact, with such exceptions and under such regulations as the Congress shall make.	No changes. Federal courts remain the only judicial body allowed to resolve disputes between the states.
The Trial of all Crimes, except in Cases of Impeachment, shall be by Jury; and such Trial shall be held in the State where the said Crimes shall have been	(3) The trial of all crimes, except in cases of impeach-ment, shall be by jury, and such trial shall be held in the State where the said crimes shall have been committed; but when not committed	No changes.

USA	CSA	Notes
committed; but when not committed within any State, the Trial shall be at such Place or Places as the Congress may by Law have directed.	within any State, the trial shall be at such place or places as the Congress may by law have directed.	
Section. 3.	**Section. 3.**	
Treason against the United States, shall consist only in levying War against them, or in adhering to their Enemies, giving them Aid and Comfort. No Person shall be convicted of Treason unless on the Testimony of two Witnesses to the same overt Act, or on Confession in open Court.	(1) Treason against the Confederate States shall consist only in levying war against them, or in adhering to their enemies, giving them aid and comfort. No person shall be convicted of treason unless on the testimony of two witnesses to the same overt act, or on confession in open court.	No changes.
The Congress shall have Power to declare the Punishment of Treason, but no Attainder of Treason shall work Corruption	(2) The Congress shall have power to declare the punish-ment of treason; but no attainder of treason shall work corruption of blood, or forfeiture, except	No changes.

USA	CSA	Notes
of Blood, or Forfeiture except during the Life of the Person attainted.	during the life of the person attainted.	
Article IV		
Section. 1.	**Section. 1.**	
Full Faith and Credit shall be given in each State to the public Acts, Records, and judicial Proceedings of every other State. And the Congress may by general Laws prescribe the Manner in which such Acts, Records and Proceedings shall be proved, and the Effect thereof.	(1) Full faith and credit shall be given in each State to the public acts, records, and judicial proceedings of every other State; and the Congress may, by general laws, prescribe the manner in which such acts, records, and proceedings shall be proved, and the effect thereof.	No changes. The CSA still forces states to recognize the court rulings of other states.
Section. 2.	**Section. 2.**	
The Citizens of each State shall be entitled to all Privileges and Immunities of Citizens in the several States.	(1) The citizens of each State shall be entitled to all the privileges and immunities of citizens in the several States; and shall have the right of transit and sojourn in any State of this Confederacy, with their slaves and other property; and the right of	Solidifying the right to slavery further, the CSA adds that government cannot prohibit the rights of individuals to haul their slaves around the country as they so please, thereby eliminating the possibility of another Dred Scott-style lawsuit.

USA	CSA	Notes
	property in said slaves shall not be thereby impaired.	
A Person charged in any State with Treason, Felony, or other Crime, who shall flee from Justice, and be found in another State, shall on Demand of the executive Authority of the State from which he fled, be delivered up, to be removed to the State having Jurisdiction of the Crime.	(2) A person charged in any State with treason, felony, or other crime against the laws of such State, who shall flee from justice, and be found in another State, shall, on demand of the executive authority of the State from which he fled, to be removed to the State having jurisdiction of the crime.	CSA does a bit of odd meddling with this clause. By adding the qualifier "against the laws of such state" they seem to be implying that only criminals accused of a *state* offense can be extradited from one state to another. So if a guy committed a federal offense he could presumably *not* be extradited in this manner.
No Person held to Service or Labour in one State, under the Laws thereof, escaping into another, shall, in Consequence of any Law or Regulation therein, be discharged from such Service or Labour, but shall be delivered up on Claim of the Party to whom such Service or Labour may be due.	(3) No slave or other person held to service or labor in any State or Territory of the Confederate States, under the laws thereof, escaping or lawfully carried into another, shall, in consequence of any law or regulation therein, be discharged from such service or labor; but shall be delivered up on claim of the party to whom such slave	In both constitutions, this clause was supposed to prevent slaves from escaping into freedom in another state.

The Confederates strengthen and clarify the language, though this is somewhat pointless since Article I, Sec. 9(4) already prevents states from passing "any law or regulation" that could possibly result in a slave becoming free by moving/being moved to a different state. |

USA	CSA	Notes
	belongs, or to whom such service or labor may be due.	
Section. 3.	**Section. 3.**	
New States may be admitted by the Congress into this Union; but no new State shall be formed or erected within the Jurisdiction of any other State; nor any State be formed by the Junction of two or more States, or Parts of States, without the Consent of the Legislatures of the States concerned as well as of the Congress.	(1) Other States may be admitted into this Confederacy by a vote of two-thirds of the whole House of Representatives and two-thirds of the Senate, the Senate voting by States; but no new State shall be formed or erected within the jurisdiction of any other State, nor any State be formed by the junction of two or more States, or parts of States, without the consent of the Legislatures of the States concerned, as well as of the Congress.	The Confederates make it a bit harder for new states to join their country, by requiring a vote of approval by a two-thirds majority vote in the House of Representatives, and a two-thirds vote in the Senate (with each state having only one vote). In the US it just takes a simple majority.
The Congress shall have Power to dispose of and make all needful Rules and Regulations respecting the Territory or other Property belonging to the United	(2) The Congress shall have power to dispose of and make all needful rules and regulations concerning the property of the Confederate States, including the lands	The language in this clause is simplified a bit in the CSA version. In both versions the federal government is given jurisdiction over the physical lands and property possessed by the country. The CSA does not promise that their

USA	CSA	Notes
States; and nothing in this Constitution shall be so construed as to Prejudice any Claims of the United States, or of any particular State.	thereof.	constitution is free of prejudice towards specific property claims.
N/A	3) The Confederate States may acquire new territory; and (Congress shall have power to legislate and provide governments for the inhabitants of all territory belonging to the Confederate States, lying without the limits of the several States [sic]; and may permit them, at such times, and in such manner as it may by law provide, to form States to be admitted into the Confederacy. In all such territory the institution of negro slavery, as it now exists in the Confederate States, shall be recognized and protected be Congress and by the Territorial	Another new clause created for the Confederacy. Like the United States, the CSA creates two tiers of local self-government in its federal system: territories and states. This clause simply clarifies that slavery is legal in the former as well as the latter, an issue that had often been debated in the antebellum United States.

USA	CSA	Notes
	government; and the inhabitants of the several Confederate States and Territories shall have the right to take to such Territory any slaves lawfully held by them in any of the States or Territories of the Confederate States.	
The United States shall guarantee to every State in this Union a Republican Form of Government, and shall protect each of them against Invasion; and on Application of the Legislature, or of the Executive (when the Legislature cannot be convened), against domestic Violence.	(4) The Confederate States shall guarantee to every State that now is, or hereafter may become, a member of this Confederacy, a republican form of government; and shall protect each of them against invasion; and on application of the Legislature or of the Executive (when the Legislature is not in session) against domestic violence.	No real changes. The federal government retains the right to deploy troops to states when asked.
	Article V	
Section. 1.	**Section. 1.**	
The Congress, whenever two thirds of both Houses shall deem it necessary, shall	(1) Upon the demand of any three States, legally assembled in their several conven-	The CSA method for making constitutional amendments is a bit different, but keeps the general spirit intact. The

USA	CSA	Notes
propose Amendments to this Constitution, or, on the Application of the Legislatures of two thirds of the several States, shall call a Convention for proposing Amendments, which, in either Case, shall be valid to all Intents and Purposes, as Part of this Constitution, when ratified by the Legislatures of three fourths of the several States, or by Conventions in three fourths thereof, as the one or the other Mode of Ratification may be proposed by the Congress; Provided that no Amendment which may be made prior to the Year One thousand eight hundred and eight shall in any Manner affect the first and fourth Clauses in the Ninth Section of the first Article; and that no State, without its Consent, shall be deprived of its equal Suffrage	tions, the Congress shall summon a convention of all the States, to take into consideration such amendments to the Constitution as the said States shall concur in suggesting at the time when the said demand is made; and should any of the proposed amendments to the Constitution be agreed on by the said convention — voting by States — and the same be ratified by the Legislatures of two-thirds of the several States, or by conventions in two-thirds thereof — as the one or the other mode of ratification may be proposed by the general convention — they shall thenceforward form a part of this Constitution. But no State shall, without its consent, be deprived of its equal represent-ation in the Senate.	biggest difference is that in the Confederacy the Congress has no role in passing amendments. It's all done by the state legislatures. In the CSA system it only takes three states to summon a constitutional convention, where as in the US it takes the request of "two-thirds" of them. Likewise, in the CSA it only takes two-thirds of the states to ratify an amendment, while in the US it takes three-fourths. Lastly, the CSA changes the final rule. In the US a state cannot be deprived of its equal *suffrage* in the Senate, but under the Confederacy it cannot be denied equal *representation*. So theoretically CSA states could be given different voting powers so long as they all have the same number of senators.

USA	CSA	Notes
in the Senate.		
Article VI		
Section. 1.	**Section. 1.**	
N/A	1. The Government established by this Constitution is the successor of the Provisional Government of the Confederate States of America, and all the laws passed by the latter shall continue in force until the same shall be repealed or modified; and all the officers appointed by the same shall remain in office until their successors are appointed and qualified, or the offices abolished.	The CSA indicates it has legal continuity with its previous provisional government.
All Debts contracted and Engagements entered into, before the Adoption of this Constitution, shall be as valid against the United States under this Constitution, as under the Confederation.	2. All debts contracted and engagements entered into before the adoption of this Constitution shall be as valid against the Confederate States under this Constitution, as under the Provisional Government.	No changes.
This Constitution, and the Laws of the	3. This Constitution, and	No changes, except that

USA	CSA	Notes
United States which shall be made in Pursuance thereof; and all Treaties made, or which shall be made, under the Authority of the United States, shall be the supreme Law of the Land; and the Judges in every State shall be bound there-by, any Thing in the Constitution or Laws of any State to the Contrary notwithstanding.	the laws of the Confederate States made in pursuance thereof, and all treaties made, or which shall be made, under the authority of the Confederate States, shall be the supreme law of the land; and the judges in every State shall be bound thereby, anything in the constitution or laws of any State to the contrary notwithstanding.	the CSA inexplicably gets rid of the words "which shall be" in the first sentence.
The Senators and Representatives before mentioned, and the Members of the several State Legislatures, and all executive and judicial Officers, both of the United States and of the several States, shall be bound by Oath or Affirmation, to support this Constitution; but no religious Test shall ever be required as a Qualification to any Office or public Trust under the United States.	4. The Senators and Representatives before mentioned, and the members of the several State Legislatures, and all executive and judicial officers, both of the Confederate States and of the several States, shall be bound by oath or affirmation to support this Constitution; but no religious test shall ever be required as a qualification to any office or public trust under the	No changes.

USA	CSA	Note
	Confederate States.	
[Amendment IX] The enumeration in the Constitution, of certain rights, shall not be construed to deny or disparage others retained by the people.	5. The enumeration, in the Constitution, of certain rights shall not be construed to deny or disparage others retained by the people of the several States.	The last two amendments from the US Bill of Rights are incorporated into the end of the CSA constitution.
[Amendment X] The powers not delegated to the United States by the Constitution, nor prohibited by it to the States, are reserved to the States respectively, or to the people.	6. The powers not delegated to the Confederate States by the Constitution, nor prohibited by it to the States, are reserved to the States, respectively, or to the people thereof.	No changes.
Article VII		
Section. 1.	**Section. 1.**	
The Ratification of the Conventions of nine States, shall be sufficient for the Establishment of this Constitution between the States so ratifying the Same.	1. The ratification of the conventions of five States shall be sufficient for the establishment of this Constitution between the States so ratifying the same.	Both constitutions' Article VII has to do with how the constitution is adopted.
N/A	2. When five States shall have ratified this Constitution, in the manner before specified, the Congress under the Provisional Constitution shall	The CSA established a provisional constitution immediately after its founding. That document was to continue to be used until the interim Congress could set an election date for the election of a new,

USA	CSA	Notes
	prescribe the time for holding the election of President and Vice President; and for the meeting of the Electoral College; and for counting the votes, and inaugurating the President. They shall, also, prescribe the time for holding the first election of members of Congress under this Constitution, and the time for assembling the same. Until the assembling of such Congress, the Congress under the Provisional Constitution shall continue to exercise the legislative powers granted them; not extending beyond the time limited by the Constitution of the Provisional Government.	permanent Congress and president. This day never came. This constitution was never used.

SUMMARY

By J.J. McCullough

Overall, the CSA constitution does not radically alter the federal system that was established by the United States constitution. It is therefore very debatable as to whether the CSA was a significantly more pro-"states' rights" country (as supporters claim) in any meaningful sense. At least three states rights are explicitly taken *away* — the freedom of states to grant voting rights to non-citizens, the freedom of states to trade freely with each other, and of course the freedom of states to outlaw slavery within their borders.

States only *gain* four minor rights under the Confederate system — the power to enter into treaties with other states to regulate waterways, the power to tax foreign and domestic ships that *use* their waterways, the power to impeach federally-appointed state officials, and the power to distribute "bills of credit."

As previously noted, the CSA constitution does not modify many of the most controversial (from a states' rights perspective) clauses of the American constitution, including the "Supremacy" clause (Art. VI, Sec. 1[3]), the "Commerce" clause (Art. I, Sec. 8[3]) and the "Necessary and Proper" clause (Art. I, Sec. 8[18]). Nor does the CSA take away the federal government's right to suspend *habeus corpus* or "suppress insurrections."

As far as slave-owning rights go, however, the document is much more effective. Four different clauses entrench the legality of slavery in a number of different ways, and together they virtually guarantee that *any* sort of anti-slave law or policy would be unconstitutional. People can claim the Civil War was "not about slavery" as much as they want, but the fact remains that anyone who fought for the Confederacy was fighting for a country in which a universal right to own slaves was one of the most entrenched laws of the land.

In the end, however, many of the most interesting changes introduced in the CSA constitution have nothing to do with federalism or slavery at all. The president's term limit and line-item veto, along with the various fiscal restraints, and the ability of cabinet members to answer questions on the floor of Congress are all innovative, neutral ideals whose merits may still be worth pondering today.

Appendix C – Louis Nelson Pension File

No. **32** ACCEPTED

STATE OF TENNESSEE

Colored Man's Application for Pension

Louis Nelson

Co. 7 Tenn Cav Rgt.

Filed June 25. 21

Allowed

Card June 25. 21

Died August 26-1934.

NOTICE, APPLICANTS.

The Negroes' pension law passed by the Tennessee Legislature, provides that the Negroes pensioned by this Act must have been actual *bona fide* residents of this State three years if they served with a Tennessee command, and ten years if they served with a command from any other State. They must have remained with the army until the close of the war, unless legally relieved from service. They must be indigent. Unless you come clearly under the law, it is useless to file an application.

The Board meets the second Tuesdays in January, April, July and October.

All blanks on this filing to be filled by the Pension Board.

FOSTER & PARKES CO., NASHVILLE.

Ripley R1

137

Print Image https://familysearch.org/pal:/MM9.3.1/TH-1951-20617-2640-25...

Tennessee, Confederate Pe...ers and Widows, 1891-1965 > Colored Troops > no 1-285 > Image 273 of 2629 >

Colored Man's Application for Pension.

I, *Louis Neeson* .... a native of the State of *Tennessee* and now a citizen of Tennessee, resident at *Ripley* .... in the County of *Lauderdale* in said State of Tennessee, and who was a servant from the State of *Tennessee* .... in the war between the United States and the Confederate States, do hereby apply for aid under the Act of the General Assembly of Tennessee, of 1921. And I do solemnly swear that I was with *E R Oldham + Sidney Oldham, in Co. "M" 7th Tennessee Cavalry* in the service of the Confederate States, and that by reason of indigence I am now entitled to receive the benefit of this Act. I further swear that I do not hold any National, State or county office, nor do I receive aid or pension from any other State, or from the United States. I do further solemnly swear that the answers given to the following questions are true:

In what County, State and year were you born?

Answer *Lauderdale County Tennessee*

When did you go with the army? Give the names of the regimental and company officers under whom your master served.

Answer *Col. Duckworth Lieut Co W.F.Taylor, Capt. D.J.Davis, 7th Tenn. Cav.,*

Give the name of your owner *E R Oldham, Sidney Oldham + James Oldham*

Answer ....

What estate have you in your own right, real and personal, and what is its actual cash value?

Answer *House + Lot, Valued at $1600.00, Encumbered for $600.00 x by Trust Deed,*

What estate has your wife in her own right, real and personal, and what is its actual cash value?

Answer *She has no Estate.*

State the gross income of yourself and your wife from all sources for the past year. This must include all money received either

Questions from the North; Answers from the South – James R. Elstad

from wages, rents or interest on loaned money, if any. Also family supplies raised or received from rents and used by your family.

Answer About $300.00 per year, gross income of self + wife. & We are in debt for our home & trying to pay it out of debt & it takes all we earn to live on.

How long and since when have you been an actual resident of the State of Tennessee?

Answer All of my life

Have you an attorney to look after this application?

Answer Yes

If so, give his name and address.

Answer Nicolaus Steve Ripley Tenn. No fee charged —

Witness my hand this 14 day of June 1921

WITNESSES

E. R. Oldham .... Witness.

Postoffice Address Ripley Tenn

O. A. Mallison ...... Witness.

Postoffice Address Ripley Tenn R#5

Louis X Nelson
his
mark

Street and No., if any

P. O. R. F. D. No-1-

R. F. D. (if any)

139

Questions from the North; Answers from the South – James R. Elstad

Print Image https://familysearch.org/pal:/MM9.3.1/TH-1951-20617-2342-64...

Tennessee, Confederate Pe...ers and Widows, 1891-1965 > Colored Troops > no
1-285 > Image 276 of 2629 >

Faint Image tissue paper documents weak print

September 24, 1934.

Florence Alberta Nelson, Col.
Ripley, Tennessee.

Dear Florence:-

Your application for pension has been sent to this office by
Honorable Roy C. Wallace, State Comptroller, for attention.

In examining your papers, however, I find that your husband,
Louis Nelson, was an ex-servant during the Civil War and drew a pension
until his death, August 26, 1934. Under the law you are not entitled to
apply for a pension, as the State of Tennessee only pays a pension to
Confederate Veterans, their widows, and ex-servants--no provision is
made for widows of ex-servants. I am therefore returning all papers
which you forwarded to Mr. Wallace.

Yours very truly,

Mrs. Mary B. Gamble,
G/R   Special Examiner.

CC: Honorable Roy C. Wallace,
    State Comptroller,
    State Capitol,
    Nashville, Tennessee.

CC: Mr. W. Dan Majors, Cashier,
    Ripley Savings Bank & Trust Co.,
    Ripley, Tennessee.

Faint Image tissue paper documents weak print

December 3, 1934.

Mrs. E. R. Oldham,
Route #4,
Covington, Tennessee.

Dear Mrs. Oldham:-

This will acknowledge receipt of your letter of November
27, 1934, asking for the record of Lewis (or Louis) Nelson, colored.

The records of this office show that Louis Nelson, Ripley,
Lauderdale County, Tennessee, filed an application for Colored Man's
pension June 25, 1921, under number 52, and was granted same July 12, 1921,
which he continued to draw until his death August 26, 1934.

His application states he was born in Lauderdale County,
Tennessee. He served in the Confederate Army with E. R. Oldham and Sidney
Oldham, in Company M, 7th Tennessee Cavalry, under Col. Duckworth, Lieut.
Col. W. F. Taylor, Capt. B. T. Davis. E. R. Oldham, a Confederate soldier
and pensioner, makes the following affidavit: "The applicant, Lewis Nelson,
was a cook for E. R. Oldham in Co. M, 7th Tennessee Cavalry and was with
said Company as a servant and cook at the close of the war."

I trust this is the information you desire. Of course,
you understand that there are no records in Washington of ex-servants, and
that the only records we can give you is just what is stated in his application.

Yours very truly,

Mrs. Mary B. Gamble,
G/R   Special Examiner.

142

Faint Image tissue paper documents weak print

Oct. 15, 1936

Major F.C.Simpson, Asst.
Q.M.Corps,
War Dept.
Washington, D.C.

Dear sir:

Your letter of October 14th just received,
and the information concerning Louis Napoleon Nelson,
is as follows:

" Colored Man's Application for Pension # 52.

The applicant Louis Nelson was a cook for E.A.
Oldham, in Co. M. 7th Tennessee Cavalry, and was with
said Company as a servant and cook at the close of the
war.   Signed,   E.R.Oldham,
                                         F.A.Walker, Sr.   "

Yours very truly,

Mrs. Mary B. Gamble,
Special Examiner,
Confederate Pension Board.

Faint Image tissue paper documents weak print

32
Entd.

RECEIVED

SEP 6 1934

CONFEDERATE
OFFICE
TENNESSEE

Sept 4th., 1934.

Mr. W. Dan Majors, Cashier,
Ripley Savings Bank & Trust Co.,
Ripley, Tenn.

Dear Sir:-

Lauderdale County

Your letter returning pension warrant issued Louis Nelson, colored, and advising of his death on Aug 26th.

I am enclosing herewith blank for making proof of death, which please have his widow execute and return, and warrant will be issued for balance due estate of the deceased.

It is unnecessary that she qualify as administratrix.

Very truly,

State Comptroller.

CC to Pension Board.

144

WAR DEPARTMENT
OFFICE OF THE QUARTERMASTER GENERAL
WASHINGTON

IN REPLY REFER TO QM 293 A-M
Nelson, Louis Napoleon

October 14, 1936.

Secretary, Pension Board,
War Memorial Bldg.,
Nashville, Tenn.

Dear Sir:

It would be appreciated if you would make a search of your pension files and furnish this office a statement of the military service of one Louis Napoleon Nelson, reported to have served with Co. M, 7th Tenn. Cav., C.S.A., and to have received a pension from Lauderdale County, Tennessee, until 1934.

Thanking you for your report on this case, I am

For The Quartermaster General,

Very truly yours,

F. C. SIMPSON,
Major, Q. M. Corps,
Assistant.

Incl.
Franked Env.

Residence of

E. R. OLDHAM
FARMING and LUMBER

Telephone
Ripley Exchange
No. 2621

Route 1   Henning, Tenn.,   June 29th   1921

Gent. Jno P. Dickman
Sec Board Confederate Pensions
Nashville. Tenn.

My dear Comrade:-

I suppose, before you receive this letter, you have received, from Hon. Ward State, Atty, at Ripley, the application, for a Pension, from Lewis Nelson, Colored, who was my Cook while I was a Confederate Soldier.

I shall be highly pleased if your board approves Lewis Nelson's application; because, he not only made an acceptable and faithful Cook but his Conduct, since the War between the States, has been very acceptable to all good citizens.

Your Comrade and friend
E R Oldham

146

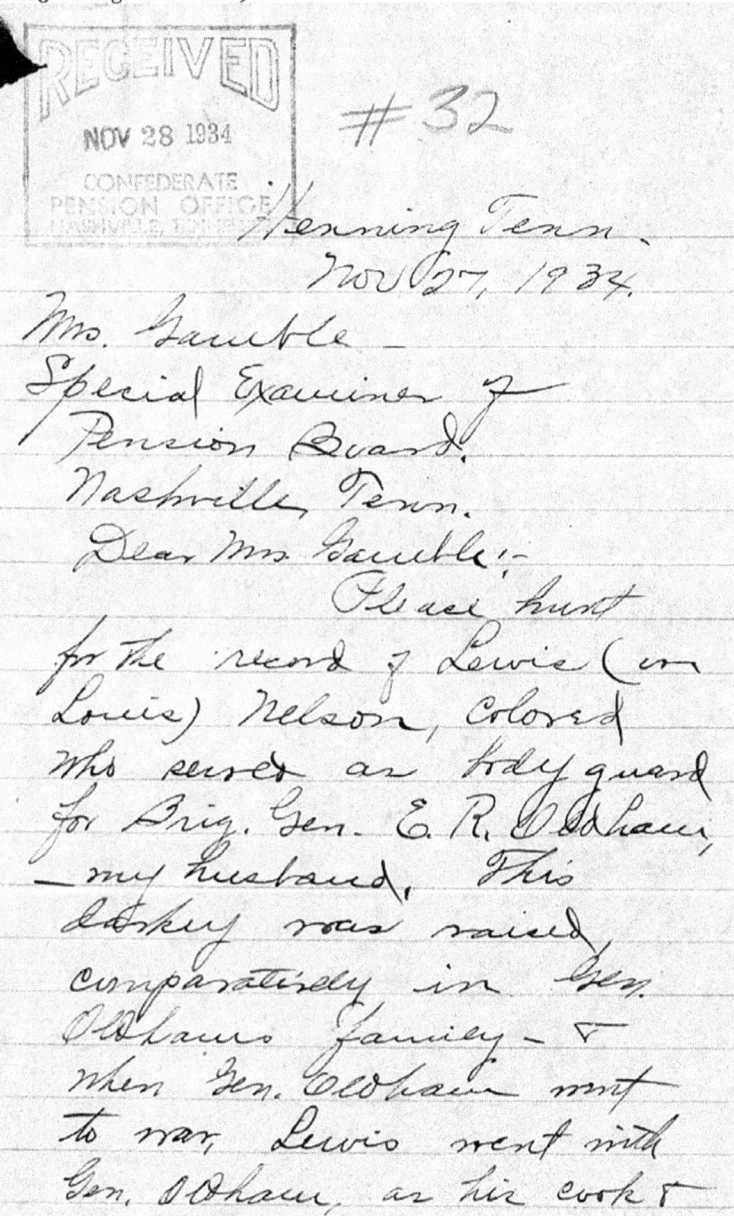

RECEIVED
NOV 28 1934
CONFEDERATE
PENSION OFFICE
NASHVILLE, TENN.

#32

Henning Tenn.
Nov 27, 1934.

Mr. Gamble –
Special Examiner of
Pension Board,
Nashville, Tenn.
      Dear Mr. Gamble:-
            Please hunt
for the record of Lewis (or
Louis) Nelson, Colored
who served as body guard
for Brig. Gen. E. R. Oldham,
– my husband, This
darkey was raised
comparatively in Gen.
Oldhams family – &
when Gen. Oldham went
to war, Lewis went with
Gen. Oldham, as his cook &

2

body guard. Recently
you sent me Gen. Oldham's
record, — from Washington.
I hope you will not
have any trouble in
finding his record.
Gen. DeSaussure thinks
it should not be a difficult
task, — since he was a
true & worthy soldier.
Certainly thank you
for your services!
Sincerely,
Mrs. E. R. Oldham.
R-4 Covington, Tenn.

Appendix D – Slavery Abolition Act 1833

NOTE: The original for this information can be found on the website below. The only changes made were to get the data into the correct format for the publisher.

http://www.saylor.org/site/wp-content/uploads/2011/05/Slavery-Abolition-Act-1833.pdf

An Act for the Abolition of Slavery throughout the British Colonies; for promoting the Industry of the manumitted Slaves; and for compensating the Persons hitherto entitled to the Services of such Slaves.
Statute book chapter: 3 & 4 Will.4 c.73

Dates Royal Assent 28 August 1833
Commencement: 1 August 1834, 1 December 1834 (Cape of Good Hope), 1 February 1835 (Mauritius)
Repeal date: 19 November 1998

Related legislation:
Slave Trade Act 1807, Slave Trade Act 1824, Slave Trade Act 1843, Slave Trade Act 1873

Repealing legislation:
Statute Law (Repeals) Act 1998
Status: Repealed
Text of statute as originally enacted

The Slavery Abolition Act 1833 (citation 3 & 4 Will. IV c. 73) was an 1833 Act of the Parliament of the United Kingdom abolishing slavery throughout most of the British Empire (with the notable exceptions "of the Territories in the Possession of the East India Company," the "Island of Ceylon," and "the Island of Saint Helena").

The Act was repealed in 1998 as part of a wider rationalisation of English statute law, but later anti-slavery legislation remains in force.

Background: Slavery had been abolished in England in 1772 and Britain had outlawed the slave trade with the Slave Trade Act in 1807, with penalties of £100 per slave levied on British captains found importing slaves (treaties signed with other nations expanded the scope of the trading ban). Small trading nations that did not have a great deal to give up, such as Sweden, quickly followed suit, as did the Netherlands, also by then a minor player, however the British empire on its own constituted a substantial fraction of the world's population. The Royal Navy established the West Africa Squadron (or Preventative Squadron) at substantial expense in 1808 after Parliament passed the Act. The squadron's task was to suppress the Atlantic slave trade by patrolling the coast of West Africa. This suppressed the slave trade but did not stop it entirely. It is possible that if slave ships were in danger of being captured by the Royal Navy, some captains may have ordered the slaves to be thrown into the sea to reduce the fines they had to pay.

Between 1808 and 1860 the West Africa Squadron captured 1,600 slave ships and freed 150,000 Africans. Notwithstanding what had been done to suppress the trade, further measures were soon discovered to be necessary.

Slavery Abolition Act 1833: The first Society for Effecting the Abolition of the Slave Trade was established in Britain in 1787, and members included John Barton; William Dillwyn; George Harrison; Samuel Hoare Jr; Joseph Hooper; John Lloyd; Joseph Woods Sr; James Phillips; Thomas Clarkson, Granville Sharp, Philip Sansom and Richard Phillips.

The later Anti-Slavery Society was founded in 1823. Members included Joseph Sturge, Thomas Clarkson, William Wilberforce, Henry Brougham, Thomas Fowell Buxton, Elizabeth Heyrick, Mary Lloyd, Jane Smeal, Elizabeth Pease, and Anne Knight.

During the Christmas holiday of 1831, a large-scale slave revolt in Jamaica known as the Baptist War broke out. It was organised originally as a peaceful strike by Baptist minister Samuel Sharpe. The rebellion was suppressed by the militia of the Jamaican plantocracy and the British garrison ten days later in early 1832. Because the loss of property and life in the 1831 rebellion, the British Parliament held two inquiries. The results of these inquiries contributed greatly to the abolition of slavery with the Slavery Abolition Act 1833.

A successor organisation to the Anti-Slavery Society was formed in 1839, committed to worldwide abolition. Its official name was the British and Foreign Anti-Slavery Society.

This continues today as Anti-Slavery International.

Main points of the Act

Slavery was officially abolished in most of the British Empire on 1 August 1834.

In practical terms, however, only slaves below the age of six were freed, as all slaves over the age of six were re-designated as "apprentices".

Apprentices would continue to serve their former owners for a period of time after the abolition of slavery, though the length of time they served depended on which of three classes of apprentice they were.

The first class of apprentices were former slaves who "in their State of Slavery were usually employed in Agriculture, or in the Manufacture of Colonial Produce or otherwise, upon Lands belonging to their Owners".

The second class of apprentices were former slaves who "in their State of Slavery were usually employed in Agriculture, or in the

Manufacture of Colonial Produce or otherwise, upon Lands not belonging to their Owners".

The third class of apprentices was composed of all former slaves "not included within either of the Two preceding Classes".

Apprentices within the third class were released from their apprenticeships on 1 August 1838.

The remaining apprentices within the first and second classes were released from their apprenticeships on 1 August 1840.

The Act also included the right of compensation for slave-owners who would be losing their property. The amount of money to be spent on the compensation claims was set at "the Sum of Twenty Millions Pounds Sterling".

Under the terms of the Act the British government raised £20 million to pay out in compensation for the loss of the slaves as business assets to the registered owners of the freed slaves. The names listed in the returns for slave compensation show that ownership was spread over many hundreds of British families, many of them of high social standing.

For example, Henry Phillpotts (then the Bishop of Exeter), in a partnership with three business colleagues, received £12,700 for 665 slaves.

The majority of men and women who were awarded compensation under the 1833 Abolition Act are listed in a Parliamentary Return, entitled Slavery Abolition Act, which is an account of all moneys awarded by the Commissioners of Slave Compensation in the Parliamentary Papers 1837-8 Vol. 48.

In all, the government paid out over 40,000 separate awards. The £20 million fund was 40% of the government's total annual expenditure.

As a notable exception to the rest of the British Empire, the Act did not "extend to any of the Territories in the Possession of the East India Company, or to the Island of Ceylon, or to the Island of Saint Helena."

On 1 August 1834, an unarmed group of mainly elderly people being addressed by the Governor at Government House in Port of Spain, Trinidad, about the new laws, began chanting: "Pas de six ans. Point de six ans" ("Not six years. No six years"), drowning out the voice of the Governor. Peaceful protests continued until a resolution to abolish apprenticeship was passed and de facto freedom was achieved. Full emancipation for all was legally granted ahead of schedule on 1 August 1838, making Trinidad the first British colony with slaves to completely abolish Slavery Abolition Act 1833.

Repeal

The Slavery Abolition Act 1833 was repealed in its entirety under the Statute Law (Repeals) Act 1998.

However, this repeal has not made slavery legal again, as sections of the Slave Trade Act 1824, Slave Trade Act 1843 and Slave Trade Act 1873 are still in force. In addition the Human Rights Act 1998 incorporates into British Law Article 4 of the
European Convention on Human Rights which prohibits the holding of persons as slaves.

References

[1]http://www.pdavis.nl/Legis_07.htm
[2]"Slavery Abolition Act 1833; Section LXIV"
(http://www.pdavis.nl/Legis_07.htm)
. 1833-08-28. . Retrieved 2008-06-03.
[3]Heward, Edmund (1979). Lord Mansfield: A Biography of William Murray 1st Earl of Mansfield 1705
–1793 Lord Chief Justice for 32 years. p.141. Chichester: Barry Rose (publishers) Ltd. ISBN 0859921638

[4]"Chasing Freedom Information Sheet"
(http://www.royalnavalmuseum.org/visit_see_victory_cfexhibition
_infosheet.htm).
Royal NavalMuseum. . Retrieved 2007-04-02.
[5]"Chasing Freedom Exhibition: the Royal Navy and the
Suppression of the Transatlantic Slave Trade"
(http://www.royalnavalmuseum.org/visit_see_victory_cfexhibition
_infosheet.htm). . Retrieved 2009-09-25.
[6]d'Anjou, Leo (1996). Social Movements and Cultural Change:
The First Abolition Campaign. Aldine de Gruyter. p. 198.
ISBN 0202305228.
[7]Slavery and abolition
(http://www.oup.com/oxforddnb/info/freeodnb/shelves/slavery/)
[8]Sharman, Anne-Marie (1993), ed., Anti-Slavery Reporter vol 13
no 8. P.35. London:Anti-Slavery International
[9]"Slavery Abolition Act 1833; Section XII"
(http://www.pdavis.nl/Legis_07.htm). 1833-08-28. . Retrieved
2008-06-03.
[10]"Slavery Abolition Act 1833; Section I"
(http://www.pdavis.nl/Legis_07.htm). 1833-08-28. . Retrieved
2008-06-03.
[11]"Slavery Abolition Act 1833; Section IV"
(http://www.pdavis.nl/Legis_07.htm). 1833-08-28. . Retrieved
2008-06-03.
[12]"Slavery Abolition Act 1833; Section VI"
(http://www.pdavis.nl/Legis_07.htm). 1833-08-28. . Retrieved
2008-06-03.
[13]"Slavery Abolition Act 1833; Section V"
(http://www.pdavis.nl/Legis_07.htm). 1833-08-28. . Retrieved
2008-06-03.
[14]"Slavery Abolition Act 1833; Section XXIV"
(http://www.pdavis.nl/Legis_07.htm). 1833-08-28. . Retrieved
2008-06-03.
[15]British Parliamentary Papers, session 1837-38 (215), volume
XLVIII. The manuscript returns and indexes to the claims are held
by TheNational Archives.
[16]Danks, John (February 28, 2007). "Devon's plantation owners"
(http://www.bbc.co.uk/devon/content/

articles/2007/02/28/abolition_devon_wealth_feature.shtml). British Broadcasting Corporation. .
[17]Dryden, John. 1992 "Pas de Six Ans!" In: Seven Slaves & Slavery: Trinidad 1777 - 1838, by Anthony de Verteuil, Port of Spain, pp.371-379.
[18]"Statute Law (Repeals) Act 1998"
(http://www.opsi.gov.uk/acts/acts1998/ukpga_19980043_en_1).
1998-11-19. . Retrieved2008-06-04.
[19]"Slavery Abolition Act 1833 (repealed 19.11.1998) (c.73)"
(http://www.opsi.gov.uk/RevisedStatutes/
Acts/ukpga/1833/cukpga_18330073_en_1). Retrieved 2009-06-19.
[20]"Slave Trade Act 1824"
(http://www.statutelaw.gov.uk/content.aspx?activeTextDocId=102
9383)
. 1824-06-24. . Retrieved 2008-06-04.
[21]"Slave Trade Act 1843"
(http://www.statutelaw.gov.uk/content.aspx?activeTextDocId=103
4738)
. 1843-08-24. . Retrieved 2008-06-04.
[22]"Slave Trade Act 1873"
(http://www.statutelaw.gov.uk/content.aspx?activeTextDocId=105
2596)
. 1873-08-05. . Retrieved 2008-06-04.
[23]"Human Rights Act 1998"
(http://www.statutelaw.gov.uk/legResults.aspx?LegType=All
Primary

External links
The Parliamentary Archives holds the original of this historic record (http://www.parliament.uk/archives)
Text of the Slavery Abolition Act 1833
(http://www.pdavis.nl/Legis_07.htm)
Teaching resources about Slavery and Abolition on blackhistory4schools.com
(http://www.blackhistory4schools.com/slavetrade/)

Article Sources and Contributors
Slavery Abolition Act 1833
Source: http://en.wikipedia.org/w/index.php?oldid=425575399

Contributors: 2help, AaronRivers, Adgfs, Ahoerstemeier, Allissonn, AmandaFrench, AmyzzXX, Arthena, BillFlis, Black85ball, Blahblah13, Brunnock, Bryan Derksen, Bucketsofg, Chris the speller, Cmichael, Courcelles, Cquick100, Danlyndon, David Underdown, Delirium, Dhodges, Dogposter, ElationAviation, GGrannum, Glane23, Gonzo fan2007, Good Olfactory, Grover cleveland, HappyInGeneral, HexaChord, Howcheng, Iridescent, J.delanoy, Jcchat66, John Hill, John of Reading, Johnleemk, Joren, Kbservices, Keith-264, KelvinMo, Kurando, Law, Legis, LittlebutBIG, Lstapley, Lycurgus, Maralia, Mini12, MitchTurner84, Mrfish1200, Neddyseagoon, Nev1, Newyorkbrad, Orphan Wiki, Patton123, Piledhigheranddeeper, Punctillio, Regan123, RetiredUser2, Riana, Rich Farmbrough, Rjm at sleepers, Rjwilmsi, Road Wizard, Rror, Rst20xx, Salviogiuliano, Sannse, Savidan, Scott5114, ScottDavis, Shane Down Under, Shanes, Shentonc, Snigbrook, Solicitr, StiffyAdams, Tabletop, TerryCately, The PIPE, The Thing That Should Not Be, Thedoorhinge, Tide rolls, Tim!, Tregoweth, UberMan5000, Uncle Dick, Victuallers, Warren, Yeti Hunter, 152 anonymous edits

Bibliography

Baker, Charles E. Dr. The Christian Character of Robert E. Lee (DVD); Southern Historical Review, 652 16th Ave NW Birmingham, Alabama 35215

Cooper, William J. Jr. Jefferson Davis, American; Vintage Civil War Press

Eanes, Greg Virginia's Black Confederates, Essays and Rosters, Eanes Group, LLC, Crewe, VA 2014

Griffith, Michael T. A Southern View of the Civil War (DVD); Southern Historical Review, 2007

Lenzini, Russell; The Real Flag of the KKK,
©1995; http://www.rulen.com/kkk/

Lott, Stanley K. The American Flag is the Real Slave Flag, SKL Publications, 2005, 2015

Lott, Stanley K. Slavery and the U.S. Government, SKL Publications, 2005

McCullough, J.J.; jjmccullough.com/CSA.htm; Constitution of the Confederate States of America, What was changed? And Why?

Saylor; http://www.saylor.org/site/wp-content/uploads/2011/05/ Slavery-Abolition-Act-1833.pdf

Seabrook, Lochlainn, The Quotable Robert E. Lee, Sea Raven Press, 2011

Seabrook, Lochlainn, Everything You Were Taught About the American Slavery is Wrong, Ask A Southerner!, Sea Raven Press, 2010

Smith, Dr. Edward C.; DVD: Black Confederates, 1993; Dixie Rising, Morgantown, GA

Traywick, H.V. Jr. Empire of the Owls, Dementi Milestone Publishing Inc, 2013

Winbush, Nelson, DVD: Blacks In the Confederate Army, 1993; Dixie Depot, Dawsonville, GA

Endnotes:

---

[i] Page 1, personal correspondence from Lochlainn Seabrook.

[ii] Page 6, What Was The War Of 1861-1865 All About? H.V. Traywick

[iii] Page 6, What Was The War Of 1861-1865 All About? H.V. Traywick

[iv] Page 6, What Was The War Of 1861-1865 All About? H.V. Traywick

[v] Interview with Chief Donald Rogers, at the Catawba Tribal Headquarters, December 2010

[vi] A Southern View of the Civil War (Griffith, Michael T. © 2007 all rights reserved)

[vii] A Southern View of the Civil War (Griffith, Michael T. © 2007 all rights reserved); he quoted: Anne Farrow, Joel Lang, and Jenifer Frank wrote a book: "Complicity: How the North Promoted, Prolonged, and Profited from Slavery (New York: Ballantine Books, 2006).

[viii] See Appendix 1

[ix] What Was The War of 1861-1865 All About?; by H. V. Traywick, Jr.

[x] Lott, Stanley K; "Lincoln and the U.S. Government (The Stone Cold Facts)," unpublished manuscript, page 12

[xi] Excerpt from a "Flipboard" article which reviewed Ira Berlin's book: Generations of Captivity: A History of African-American Slaves; Harvard University Press.

[xii] Mr. Lochlainn Seabrook, "Everything You Want to Know about Slavery, Ask a Southerner"

[xiii] Lott, Stanley K; "Lincoln and the U.S. Government (The Stone Cold Facts)," unpublished manuscript, page 11

[xiv] Congressional Globe – 36th Congress, 2nd Session – Image # 357 – Year 1861. (NOTE: All Congressional Globe references came from Mr. Stanley Lott.)

[xv] United States Constitution, Article IV, Section 2, Clause 3

[xvi] Matthew 7:3-4 (NKJV)

[xvii] Discussion with Mr. Nelson Winbush, 20 July 2012

[xviii] See Appendix 1

[xix] DVD "Blacks In The Confederate Army"

[xx] Eanes, Greg; "Virginia's Black Confederates," page 33.

[xxi] Mosby, John Singleton; The Memoirs of Colonel John S. Mosby (Boston: Little, Brown and Company) 1917, p146-147. Letter to his sister Pauline dated 9 December 1862.

[xxii] Seabrook, Lochlainn; personal correspondence in response to: "Shouldn't the South pay some sort of 'Reparations" to descendants of slaves?"

[xxiii] Seabrook, Lochlainn; personal correspondence in response to: "Shouldn't the South pay some sort of 'Reparations" to descendants of slaves?"

[xxiv] A Southern View of the Civil War (Griffith, Michael T. © 2007 all rights reserved)

[xxv] Video: "Black Southern Heritage," Dr. Edward C. Smith.

[xxvi] Doug Bandow, 9 April 2015 blog: "Lessons From The Civil War 150 Years Later: U.S. Should Stop Killing People Without Good Reason."

[xxvii] Video: "Black Southern Heritage," Dr. Edward C. Smith.

[xxviii] Mr. Lochlainn Seabrook, personal correspondence.

[xxix] Mr. Lochlainn Seabrook, personal correspondence.

[xxx] Mr. Lochlainn Seabrook, personal correspondence.

[xxxi] Mr. Michael T. Griffith, "A Southern View of the Civil War."

[xxxii] Video: "Black Southern Heritage," Dr. Edward C. Smith.

[xxxiii] Video: "Black Southern Heritage," Dr. Edward C. Smith.

[xxxiv] Video: "Black Southern Heritage," Dr. Edward C. Smith.

[xxxv] Video: "Black Southern Heritage," Dr. Edward C. Smith.

[xxxvi] Congressional Globe – 36th Congress – 2nd Session – Image #1470 – bottom of left column – March 18, 1861.

[xxxvii] Congressional Globe – 36th Congress – 2nd Session – Image

[xxxviii] The Christian Character of Robert E. Lee (audio recording by Dr. Charles E. Baker).

[xxxix] A Southern View of the Civil War, Griffith, Michael T. © 2007 all rights reserved.

[xl] A Southern View of the Civil War, Griffith, Michael T. © 2007 all rights reserved.

[xli] A Southern View of the Civil War, Griffith, Michael T. © 2007 all rights reserved.

[xlii] A Southern View of the Civil War, Griffith, Michael T. © 2007 all rights reserved.

[xliii] A Southern View of the Civil War, Griffith, Michael T. © 2007 all rights reserved.

[xliv] A Southern View of the Civil War, Griffith, Michael T. © 2007 all rights reserved.

[xlv] A Southern View of the Civil War, Griffith, Michael T. © 2007 all rights reserved.

[xlvi] A Southern View of the Civil War, Griffith, Michael T. © 2007 all rights reserved.

[xlvii] Federalist Papers No. 39

[xlviii] A Southern View of the Civil War, Griffith, Michael T. © 2007 all rights reserved.

[xlix] A Southern View of the Civil War, Griffith, Michael T. © 2007 all rights reserved.

[l] A Southern View of the Civil War, Griffith, Michael T. © 2007 all rights reserved. Griffith referenced Horace Greeley's editorial in the New York Tribune, November 9, 1860.

[li] A Southern View of the Civil War, Griffith, Michael T. © 2007 all rights reserved. Griffith referenced Historian Henry C. Perkins (see quote listed below).

[lii] Historian Henry C. Perkins; Northern Editorials on Secession, Gloucester, Massachusetts: Peter Smith Publishers, 1964, p.10.

[liii] Mr. Lochlainn Seabrook, personal correspondence.

[liv] Mr. Lochlainn Seabrook, personal correspondence.

[lv] Historian Henry C. Perkins; Northern Editorials on Secession, Gloucester, Massachusetts: Peter Smith Publishers, 1964, p.10.

[lvi] A Southern View of the Civil War, (Griffith, Michael T. © 2007 all rights reserved).

[lvii] A Southern View of the Civil War, (Griffith, Michael T. © 2007 all rights reserved).

[lviii] A Southern View of the Civil War, (Griffith, Michael T. © 2007 all rights reserved).

[lix] What Was The War of 1861-1865 All About?; by H. V. Traywick, Jr.

[lx] What Was The War of 1861-1865 All About?; by H. V. Traywick, Jr.

161

[lxi] Cooper, William J. Jr; Jefferson Davis, American; Vintage Civil War Press; pg 415

[lxii] Southern View of The Civil War; Griffith, Michael T.; DVD

[lxiii] Southern View of The Civil War; Griffith, Michael T.; DVD

[lxiv] Southern View of The Civil War; Griffith, Michael T.; DVD

[lxv] Written response of Stanley Lott and in person interview on 23 July 2015

[lxvi] Southern View of The Civil War; Griffith, Michael T.; DVD

[lxvii] Congressional Globe – 36th Congress, 2nd session – Image #748 February, 1861

[lxviii] Mr. Antoine Fletcher, phone interview on 6 October 2015.

[lxix] Mr. Frank Barnes; Fort Sumter: Anvil of War, pages: 10-13

[lxx] Christopher Dickey blog Lost Causality, The Civil War's Dirty Secret: It Was Always About Slavery; 04.10.15 12:02 PM ET

[lxxi] Mr. Stanley Lott's manuscript: "Lincoln and the U.S. Government (The Stone Cold Facts) quoted the Appendix to the Congressional Globe - 32"d Congress, 1't Session – The Fugitive Slave Law, Mr. Sumner - Senate - Image #1106

[lxxii] Mr. Lochlainn Seabrook, personal correspondence.

[lxxiii] Mr. Lochlainn Seabrook, personal correspondence.

[lxxiv] Mr. Lochlainn Seabrook, personal correspondence.

[lxxv] Mr. Lochlainn Seabrook, personal correspondence.

[lxxvi] Mr. Lochlainn Seabrook, personal correspondence.

[lxxvii] Mr. Lochlainn Seabrook, personal correspondence.

[lxxviii] Mr. Lochlainn Seabrook, personal correspondence.

[lxxix] Mr. Lochlainn Seabrook, personal correspondence.

[lxxx] Mr. Lochlainn Seabrook, personal correspondence.

[lxxxi] Mr. Lochlainn Seabrook, personal correspondence.

[lxxxii] Mr. Lochlainn Seabrook, personal correspondence.

[lxxxiii] Mr. Lochlainn Seabrook, personal correspondence.

[lxxxiv] Mr. Lochlainn Seabrook, personal correspondence.

[lxxxv] Mr. Lochlainn Seabrook, personal correspondence.

[lxxxvi] Mr. Lochlainn Seabrook, personal correspondence.

[lxxxvii] Mr. Lochlainn Seabrook, personal correspondence.

[lxxxviii] Mr. Lochlainn Seabrook, personal correspondence.

[lxxxix] Mr. Lochlainn Seabrook, personal correspondence.

[xc] Discussion with Mr. Nelson Winbush, 20 July 2012
[xci] Mr. H.V. Traywick, personal correspondence.
[xcii] Mr. Lochlainn Seabrook, personal correspondence.
[xciii] Mr. H.V. Traywick, personal correspondence.
[xciv] Mr. Lochlainn Seabrook, personal correspondence.
[xcv] Mr. Lochlainn Seabrook, personal correspondence.
[xcvi] Mr. Lochlainn Seabrook, personal correspondence.
[xcvii] Mr. H.V. Traywick, personal correspondence.
[xcviii] Mr. H.V. Traywick, personal correspondence.
[xcix] Mr. H.V. Traywick, personal correspondence.
[c] Mr. H.V. Traywick, personal correspondence.
[ci] Southern Heritage.com essay titled: "General Nathan Bedford Forrest - the first true civil rights leader."
[cii] Mr. Lochlainn Seabrook, personal correspondence
[ciii] Mr. Lochlainn Seabrook, personal correspondence
[civ] Mr. Lochlainn Seabrook, personal correspondence
[cv] Mr. Lochlainn Seabrook, personal correspondence
[cvi] Lenzini, Russell; The Real Flag of the KKK, © 1995; http://www.rulen.com/kkk/
[cvii] Lenzini, Russell; The Real Flag of the KKK, © 1995; http://www.rulen.com/kkk/
[cviii] Lenzini, Russell; The Real Flag of the KKK, © 1995; http://www.rulen.com/kkk/
[cix] Lenzini, Russell; The Real Flag of the KKK, © 1995; http://www.rulen.com/kkk/
[cx] Lenzini, Russell; The Real Flag of the KKK, © 1995; http://www.rulen.com/kkk/
[cxi] Mr. Lochlainn Seabrook, personal correspondence.
[cxii] Mr. Lochlainn Seabrook, personal correspondence.
[cxiii] Mr. Lochlainn Seabrook, personal correspondence.
[cxiv] Slavery Abolition Act 1833; Section LXIV; http://www.saylor.org/site/wp-content/uploads/2011/05/Slavery-AH.V.lition-Act-1833.pdf
[cxv] Matthew 7:3 (NKJV)
[cxvi] American Colonization Society (PBS Episode: Brotherly Love, part 3 1791-1831